Cutting-Edge Technology and Libraries

NIPA GENX ELECTRONIC RESOURCES & SOLUTIONS P. LTD.
New Delhi-110 034

About the Editors

Dr. Bhanu Partap is presently working as Assistant Librarian in Nehru Library, CCS Haryana Agricultural University, Hisar (HR), India since July 2013. Before joining the current position, he has served many institutions situated in Punjab, Haryana, Uttarakhand and Chandigarh between September 2005 to July 2013. He has received MLISc. and M.A. (Mass Comm.) from Kurukshetra University, Kurukshetra and received M.Phil. (LIS) from Alagappa University, Karaikudi (Tamilnadu), India. He has passed the exam of UGC-NET in June 2010 and also received the degree of Ph.D. in Library & Information Science from Kurukshetra University, Kurukshetra. Apart from this, he has also received PGDCA, PGDJMC, and CC Yoga from Kurukshetra University, Kurukshetra. He has been awarded with Gold Medal for being University Topper in BLISc. at Kurukshetra University, Kurukshetra. He has about 16 years of professional experience in the field of librarianship. He has published about 90 articles in the National and International journals, conference proceedings and edited books, and has also written/edited 08 books. Apart from this, he has coordinated many national workshops and training programs for students, faculty and library professionals. He is also teaching one non-credit course, *i.e.*, PGS-501 (Library and Information Services) to the postgraduate and Ph.D. students of the University since 2013. He is a life member of Haryana Library Association (HLA), Indian Library Association (ILA) and Association of Agricultural Librarians and Documentalists of India (AALDI).

Dr. (Mrs.) Suniti Bala, Assistant Librarian, Punjab Agricultural University (PAU), Ludhiana , did her B.Lib.Sc. and M.Lib.Sc. from GNDU, Amritsar and Ph.D from Desh Bhagat University, Gobindgarh (Punjab). She was awarded with Gold Medal for being University Topper in B.Lib Sc. She worked as a Librarian at Attam Vallabh Jain Girls College, Sri Ganganagar, Rajasthan for five years and later in 2005, she joined as Assistant Librarian in Punjab Agricultural University, Ludhiana. She has been awarded as the best worker of the department in the year 2005 and 2006. She is Co-PI of E-GRANTH project (Strengthening of Digital Library and Information Management under NARES) in NAIP and a Nodal Officer for Organization of the departmental Libraries College of Basic Sciences, PAU; KVK, Ropar; KVK, Faridkot; KVK, Patiala. She has published more than 25 research articles and attended more than 30 seminars and conferences and delivered more than 25 lectures to train the faculty and students on the use of various databases. She is also teaching two credit courses of the university *viz* PGS 501 (Library and Information Services) and RPE-501 (Research and Publication Ethics).

Mr. Amit Kumar is presently working as Assistant Librarian at Punjab Agricultural University, Ludhiana since July 2005, before that he has worked in SLIET, Sangrur and some other institutions/ colleges in Punjab between 2002 to June 2004. He has received MLISc. (2001) from Panjab University, Chandigarh and also qualified the UGC NET exam in 2002. He has about 17 years of professional experience in the field of librarianship. He has published about 20 articles in National and International conference proceedings, Journals and edited books. He is a life member of AALDI (Association of Agricultural Librarians and Documentalists of India).

Ms. Manju is presently working as Librarian at Chandigarh College of Architecture, Chandigarh since November 2018. Prior to joining the current position, she has served Chandigarh University, Mohali (Pb.) from September 2017 to November 2018. She has received MLISc. from Maharshi Dayanand University, Rohtak, and M.Phil (LIS) from Kurukshetra University, Kurukshetra and also qualified the UGC-NET exam in January 2017. She has about 05 years of professional experience in the field of librarianship. She has published about 10 articles in National and International journals, conference proceedings, and edited books. Apart from this, she has actively participated in many conferences/seminars and workshops.

Cutting-Edge Technology and Libraries

Bhanu Partap
Assistant Librarian
Nehru Library
CCS Haryana Agricultural University
Hisar - 125 004, Haryana

Suniti Bala
Assistant Librarian
Punjab Agricultural University
Ludhiana - 141 001, Punjab

Amit Kumar
Assistant Librarian
Punjab Agricultural University
Ludhiana - 141 001, Punjab

Manju
Librarian
Chandigarh College of Architecture
Vidya Path, Sector 12 D
Chandigarh

nipa

NIPA GENX ELECTRONIC RESOURCES & SOLUTIONS P. LTD.
New Delhi-110 034

NIPA GENX ELECTRONIC RESOURCES & SOLUTIONS P. LTD.

101,103, Vikas Surya Plaza, CU Block
L.S.C.Market, Pitam Pura, New Delhi-110 034
Ph : +91 11 27341616, 27341717, 27341718
E-mail:newindiapublishingagency@gmail.com
www: www.nipabooks.com

For customer assistance, please contact
Phone: + 91-11-27 34 17 17 Fax: + 91-11- 27 34 16 16
E-Mail: feedbacks@nipabooks.com

ISBN: 978-93-94490-08-6

Composed and Designed by NIPA.

Acknowledgement

"To give thanks in solitude is enough. Thanksgiving has wings and goes where it must go. Your prayer knows much more about it than you do."

Victor Hugo

Writing or editing a book is harder than we thought and more rewarding than we could have ever imagined. None of this would have been possible without my professional friends. So this book has also been a true collaborative effort bringing together opinions and expertise from a wide range of professional friends. The contributors whose contributions have made this book see the day of light deserve a special thanks for their trust on editors, to make this book a quality contribution in the field of library sciences. At last, the editors would also like to acknowledge the efforts of NIPA, New Delhi to publish this book very nicely.

Editors

Preface

In this digital era, applications of Information and Communication Technology (ICT) have tremendously impacted every walk of human life. Information Technology (IT) has proved to be a boon for the modern society. Similarly, ICT has transformed the role of libraries creating new challenges and opportunities. ICT has an immense potential in enhancing the capabilities of libraries to increase the efficiency, productivity and effectiveness of library operations and services. Applications of ICT in libraries are becoming a key part to satisfying the ever-changing and complex informational demands of varied users' community. Another side, due to wide implementation of ICT applications in library's in-house activities as well as in services, now print information shifted to digital or electronic information. As a result of the shift of cutting-edge and emerging technologies, today's libraries are at a crossroad, facing drastic changes in many ways. Technological advances are playing a vital role in handling information explosion, to preservation and dissemination of information, to serve the users' community in many ways and to deliver the quick, easy, and quality content services up to the utmost satisfaction of the end users.

The cutting-edge technologies have impacted the library and its operations in an immense way. The technology has influenced and resolves the crucial issues related with information generation, storage, retrieval and management. The application of information and communication technology has provided great opportunities for information distribution, emphasizing on the user preference. Therefore, it is high time that the libraries have to adopt the cutting-edge technologies in the libraries for the fulfilment of the users' need on their satisfaction level.

The current volume "Cutting-Edge Technology and Libraries" is a collection of selected articles written by the library and information science professionals, teachers, and other academicians on different topics at national and international level. In this book, it has been tried to bring all the relevant issues related with the library and information services and related with the title of the book such as issues and concerns with cutting-edge technologies, challenges in promotion of e-Learning during COVID-19 pandemic, designing users friendly mobile library apps, information economy and the role of library in digital era, competent library services in academic environment and total quality management practices, MOOCS in library and information science, open educational resources in Indian perspectives, role of academic institution in promoting research integrity, ICT-Based services to the readers and access to e-resources, library consortia, and various issues and concerns related with electronic resource management, *etc.*

This book intends to serve as a reference book for all the library and information science professionals to acquaint themselves with the concept of cutting-edge technologies and its impact on libraries, and to update with the emerging or cutting-edge technologies in the field of library and information services. We hope this book will be a useful and well-rounded source of information for library and information science professionals in areas covered by the book.

The editors would also like to mention here that the views expressed in the papers contributed for this book are of the respective authors only, hence, the respective authors are fully responsible for the contents of their papers. Besides, to maintain the standard and quality of the book, all the possible efforts have been made without affecting the thought process and ideas of the authors. Views and suggestions are most welcome from the readers of the books in order to mind in future for further improvement.

Editors

Contents

List of Contributors

Abinash Dash
Librarian
Institute of Hotel Management (IHM)
Bhubaneswar, Odisha - 751 007

B. Chandrabati
MLIS, IGNOU
Bhubameswar, Odisha

Bandana Gogoi
Assistant Professor
Department of History
Biswanath College, Assam - 784 176

Bhanu Partap
Assistant Librarian
CCS Haryana Agricultural University
Hisar, Haryana - 125 004

Geetu Bala
Assistant Librarian
Chandigarh College of Architecture
Chandigarh - 160 012

Harish H.T.
Librarian
Sai Vidya Institute of Technology
Bengaluru, Karnataka - 560 064

Jitamoni Bhattacharyya
Librarian
Biswanath College, Assam - 784 176

Madhu Midha
Deputy Librarian and In-Charge (KRC)
IK Gujral Punjab Technical University
Jalandhar–Kapurthala Highway
Kapurthala, Punjab - 144 603

Manju
Librarian
Chandigarh College of Architecture
Vidya Path, Sector-12 D
Chandigarh - 160 012

Manjunatha S.R.
District Councilor
District Skill Development Office
Mandya, Karnataka - 571 401

Piyali Sarkar
Research Scholar
Department of Education
Lovely Professional University
Phagwara, Punjab - 144 402

Renu
Research Scholar
Department of Library & Information
Science, Maharshi Dayanand University
Rohtak, Haryana - 124 001

Sanjeev Kumar
Associate Librarian
Mohinder Singh Randhawa Library
Punjab Agricultural University
Ludhiana, Punjab - 141 004

Sonia Bansal
Assistant Librarian
Guru Angad Dev Veterinary and Animal
Sciences University
Ludhiana, Punjab

Sonia Sharma
Assistant Professor
Department of Education
Lovely Professional University
Phagwara, Punjab - 144 402

Sudip Bhattacharjee
Assistant Professor
Department of Library and Information Science
Maharaja BirBikram University
Agartala, Tripura

Suniti Bala
Assistant Librarian
Punjab Agricultural University
Ludhiana, Punjab

Vijay Kumar Bharati
Senior Assistant Librarian
Dr. Bhagwandas Central Library
Mahatma Gandhi Kashi Vidyapith
Varanasi, Uttar Pradesh - 221 005

Yogita Talwar
Assistant Librarian
Lovely Professional University
Jalandhar, Grand Trunk Road
Phagwara, Punjab - 144 001

1

Cutting-Edge Technologies in Libraries: Issues and Concerns

Bhanu Partap[1] and Manju[2]

[1]Nehru Library, CCS Haryana Agricultural University Hisar-125004, Haryana

[2]Chandigarh College of Architecture, Vidya Path, Sector-12 D Chandigarh-160012

ABSTRACT

With the rapid innovation in Information and Communication Technologies (ICTs), the libraries and information centres have gone through tremendous changes or facing transformation. In this digital era, libraries are facing heavy technological pressure to serve their users on their satisfaction level. Library and information professionals are also struggling more to implement these cutting-edge technologies for learning, research, and information for their users. Therefore, the library and information centres have now been trying to adopt and implementing various emerging or cutting-edge technologies in housekeeping activities as well as in its services. In this paper, an effort has been made to evaluate some of the cutting-edge technologies in libraries' point of view. An overview is also made to evaluate the concept, advantages and disadvantages of cutting-edge technologies.

Keywords: ICT, Cutting-Edge technology, Emerging technology, Library services, Impact.

1. Introduction

The rapid development of the Information and Communication Technology (ICT) has changed the entire activities of human life. Each and every person and their minute to minute activities are totally being affected by the implementation of ICT. On one side, business, trade and commerce, transportation, communication, *etc.* sectors are being affected by the use of ICT, whereas, on the other side, medical, health, banking, agriculture, education, *etc.* sectors are being affected by the implementation and use of emerging or cutting-edge technologies. Similarly, "information and communication technology has a profound impact on all spheres of activities in the libraries. Its impact has been noticed on the way the libraries are to build its collection, its technical activities, its outreach activities, its budgetary strategies, its manpower development, its infrastructural requirement and the most important its library services. With the invention of Information and Communication Technology (ICT), libraries are now using various types of emerging or cutting-edge technologies to aid the services they render. Everyday new technological advances affect the way information is handled in library information centres" (Krubu and Osawaru, 2011). Today, information is being generating hugely worldwide by the intellectuals in every field, hence, the problem is how to cope with this huge and different to control mass of information. To combat the impact of information explosion, the library professionals have developed new tools and techniques and even emerging or cutting-edge technologies are being used by the library professionals worldwide. Technological advances are playing a vital role in handling information explosion, to preservation and dissemination of information, to serve the users' community in many ways and to deliver the quick, easily, and quality content services up to the utmost satisfaction.

"The libraries of the current era are facing many challenges, as research and services are reshaping, and needs of researchers are increasing, people don't have time to visit the libraries while they want to get the desired material of their choices without wasting time. The cutting-edge technology has brought revolution in all walk of lifestyle. Similarly, libraries have also hugged this kind of technologies for the best possible services. To offer quick and quality services information to its users, the libraries are becoming trendsetter in the age of digitization, the world has become a global village and information in one corner of the world is quickly spreading in the other corner in no time" (Hussain, 2020).

The cutting-edge technologies have impacted the library and its operations in an immense way. The technology has impacted and resolves the crucial issues related with information generation, storage, retrieval and management. The application of information and communication technology has provided great opportunities for information distributed them the way and form the user preferred. Therefore, it is high time that the libraries have to adopt the cutting-edge technologies in the libraries for the fulfillment of the users need on their satisfaction level. In view of this, a study has been planned to evaluate the cutting-edge technologies, which are currently being adopted worldwide in libraries.

2. Meaning of Cutting-Edge Technology

In simple words, cutting-edge technology is a technology or technological devices and techniques, which can be used in any field of specialization for its improvement or development. Cutting-edge technology refers to current and fully developed technology features. "Cutting-edge technology refers to technological devices, techniques or achievements that employ the most current and high-level IT developments; in other words, technology at the frontiers of knowledge. Leading and innovative IT industry organizations are often referred to as 'cutting edge'. Furthermore, Cutting edge is also known as leading-edge technology or state-of-the-art technology" (Techopedia, 2022).

3. Impact of ICT or Cutting-edge Technology on Libraries and Information Services

Information and Community Technology (ICT) has widely impacted the libraries and information services. The overall working pattern and service delivery pattern of library and information centres have totally been changed with the rapid innovations in technology and its implementation in libraries and its activities. On the other hand, "information has always been prime factor for the improvement of society. The growth of information and the dependency on it have covered the way for the information society and subsequently the knowledge society. Information has become important part of our lives and should be available when needed. Information services are produced using new tools and techniques to facilitate the right users to the right information" (Eje and Dushu, 2018). Cutting-edge technology has highly affected the library and its services. "Libraries are now adapting new trends based on digital applications and artificial intelligence in the current era of information technology. As new perspectives of technology trends have highly affected different services. Similarly, libraries are a trendsetter and implementing these new technologies for their patron to provide them with access to reach the library resources and services without wasting time".

4. Advantages of Cutting-edge Technology

Some of the advantages of cutting-edge technology with regard to the use in libraries and information services are given as under:

- Information explosion
- Changing needs of users
- Impact of ICT on each and every human endeavour
- Digitization of information contents due to many benefits
- Lack of time to search the required information
- Quick and easy dissemination of information and contents
- Easy to store and retrieval of information and contents
- Need of the era

5. Disadvantages of Cutting-edge Technology

Some of the disadvantages of cutting-edge technology may be identified as given below:

- Sometime technology is looking easy to use but it's not that and required expertise, hence, proven time consuming
- Technology always requires upgrading so lot of funds and trained professionals are required, which are sometime difficult to maintain
- Every library and information centres cannot afford the expensive technology, particularly in India and developing countries
- Lot of labour and time is required to fix, correct, improve, check and update more in various options available in software and service delivery pattern
- It is very difficult to select the right technology for delivery of information to the users
- Every user may have not the skills to use the technology based information services
- Technology based services sometime cannot be based on users' choice
- Sufficient administrative and financial support sometime cannot be provided to the libraries by their concerned authorities, hence, ignorance towards the use of technology may develop in the library professionals

6. Popular Cutting-edge Technologies Adopting in Libraries Worldwide

There are numerous technologies being adopted by librarians or library professionals worldwide in their library services in order to satisfy the needs of their present and prospective users. Some of the popular cutting-edge technologies are analyzed as follows:

Artificial Intelligence

According to **Britannica** online academic edition, "**Artificial Intelligence (AI)** is the ability of a digital computer or computer-controlled robot to perform tasks commonly associated with intelligent beings". In this digital era, artificial intelligence is gaining more attraction and incorporation in our daily routine activities as this application focuses on delivering information to the users. Application of AI is now adopting worldwide in library services and libraries are trying to connect the users with their needed information easily and effectively. However, it is also stated about AI, that intelligence is artificial, not human. By adopting AI in libraries, information services can be provided in better way but libraries cannot establish the human or emotional relations with users. Adding an intelligent side to all applications at the library is a real opportunity to understand the patterns in user behaviour and adapt to their needs.

Augmented Reality

Augmented Reality (AR) is an interactive experience of a real-world environment whereby the objects that reside in the real-world are augmented by computer-generated perceptual information. Augmented Reality has the potential to bridge the gap between electronic and physical resources within the library. Some of the practical applications of Augmented Reality could be implemented in libraries such as shelf-reading and inventory applications, marketing methods, and location services.

Block-Chain Technology

Sue Alman, a teacher of emerging technologies elaborate that "Blockchain technology represents a decentralized database that keeps records of pseudonymized digital transactions that are visible to anyone within the network. Therefore, it is a new way to collect and store data. Blockchain has a number of other potential applications in information science. It could be used to build an enhanced metadata system for libraries and data centres, to keep track of digital-first sale rights and ownership, to connect networks of libraries and universities, or even to support community-based borrowing and skill sharing programs".

Virtual Reality

Virtual reality as the name shows that the things will be done in virtual environment but just like real or happened around us. Virtual reality can be used to bring the library closer to the users by creating virtual tours of the library or even virtual workshops and training. The social media of the future will be more than just a web page; it will be a world of its own. Status updates, news stories all will be experienced rather than just read.

Big Data

About the use of big data in libraries, Ginny Mies (2016) emphasizes that "libraries can use core customer intelligence to better reach customers, create a better connection with the community and become more relevant and stay more flexible and adaptable to all the environment changes". Furthermore, libraries can use big data to create a personalized user experience by offering content and resources based on each individual wish. But at the same time, libraries must consider the privacy issues coming with any access to personal data.

Internet of Things (IoT)

"Internet of Things (IoT) is an ultimate technology to influence the users by providing efficient services faster and convenient. The proposed technologies, Cloud computing, Magic Mirror, Pressure sensor pads through wireless sensor networks can increase profitability by improving resources utilization and development of management services in the academic libraries" (Pujar and Satyanarayana, 2015, p. 187). In other words, "the modern libraries adjust Internet of Things in different segments such as smart building technology for example cooling, heating and lighting can be controlled from smart phones app under this technology. It can also be used for people countering in different section of the library".

Robots

Robots or robotics technology is now being implemented in many areas such as industries, hospitals, defence, communication, hotels, entertainment, and libraries as well. Robots have great value in library services and many developed countries are currently using robots to serve the users' such as book delivery, searching documents, reference services, *etc.*

Drones

The small flying electronic device, which are remotely controlled are called drone. Drone technology is the latest innovation and are being utilized in many sectors. Similarly, in libraries, the "drones can be used for creating content for the library or collecting data. The drone can be used for delivery service for the library users who don't have the possibility to go the library" especially for peoples with disability, senior citizens and the peoples staying at long distances to the library.

3D Printers

3D printing service has now been adopting as cutting-edge technology in libraries and is becoming more popular these days as the charges of 3D printing are going cheaper with the passage of time. "It is assuming that the library could provide access to appropriate modeling software along with staff support; a 3D printer could enable and support rapid prototyping of experimental apparatuses and custom parts". 3D printing uses Computer-Aided Design (CAD) to create three-dimensional objects through a layering method.

User focused Interfaces and Application

Libraries are in transactional phase, hence, to maintain its value or existence, the libraries have to adopt user focused or user centred approaches. "One of the future perspectives of library services is a personalized interaction between the system and the user. Whether this is an interactive game projected onto the floor for children to interact with, digital exhibitions featured on screens, big screens in libraries that can be used to offer different kinds of information and also inspire users to find certain books or a simple display that allows taking a 'selfie'; libraries can use technology to create a digital experience for the user".

Federated Search

The new generation technology or web-savvy users prefer single search box approach offered by search engines like Google or Yahoo, *etc.*, that serve as a single-window access interface for all web-based resources. Kumar *et al.* (2008) explained that "federated searching (also known as meta-searching or cross-database searching) is a technology that allows users to search many networked information sources from one interface. Federated searching allows users to search across a number of information resources simultaneously". The federated search solutions facilitate users to search multiple full-text and bibliographic databases subscribed by the library as well as open access e-resources, library OPAC, Institutional Repositories (IR), *etc.* information resources through a single search box.

Library Mobile Apps

"Mobile apps are a real trend right now, as people have access to their mobile devices constantly. A mobile app can extend the library's services outside their physical borders and facilitate the interaction with patrons. An mobile app can facilitating library activities such as library catalogue, interactive library guides, a library virtual tour, an interactive calendar with all the library's events, the possibility to loan and read electronic books and articles, the possibility to reserve the library's resources or to pay for some services represent a real benefit for the patrons" (Princh, 2018).

Cloud Computing

"Cloud computing is a technology that uses the web (Internet) and central remote servers to maintain data, software and application. Cloud computing allows users to use applications without installation in their local machine to access their personal and official files on any computer with Internet access" (Waljat, 2018). Most of the libraries particularly higher educational institutions libraries and research libraries tried to offer cloud based services, which means services are offered through Internet/network such as OCLC, Shodhganga, AgriCat, Krishikosh repositories, *etc.*

7. Conclusion

Information and Communication Technology (ICT) has changed the overall information delivery pattern worldwide. Libraries are now totally been shifted from traditional form to digital form. Library users and other information stakeholders usually have not sufficient time to visit the library personally on frequent basis to access their needed information. The emerging or cutting-edge technologies have highly affected the users as well as the library. To fulfil the informational requirements of the users', now it is trying by the libraries to serve their users' community on their doorstep or as per their convenience. Cutting-edge technology has affected the information delivery pattern and proves beneficial for libraries as well as for users. Technology enhances the effectiveness and quality of libraries and information services. Therefore, an overview about some of the main cutting-edge technologies is given in this paper, which can be useful for the library professionals and for all the informational stakeholders to understand the cutting-edge technologies, which can be implemented in the libraries to serve the users in utmost satisfaction level.

References

Alman, Sue (2018). Blockchain in the libraries. https://www.edsurge.com/news/2018-02-01-blockchain-in-the-library-researchers-explore-potential-applications

Artificial intelligence (2022). https://www.britannica.com/technology/artificial-intelligence/ Nouvelle-AI

Chaurasia, Neeraj (2014). Emerging technologies for library management and services. New Delhi: Ess Ess Publications, 295p.

Cutting-Edge Technology (2022). https://www.techopedia.com/definition/26589/cutting-edge-technology#:~:text=Cutting%2Dedge%20technology%20refers%20to, to%20as %20% 22cutting%20edge.%22

Eje, Ogar Christopher, & Dushu, Tangkat Yusuf (2018). Transforming library and information services delivery using innovation technologies. *Library Philosophy and Practice (e-journal),* Paper no. 2036. http://digitalcommons.unl.edu/libphilprac/2036

Husain, Abid (2020). Cutting edge: Technology's impact on library service. File:/// G:\Cutting-Edge_-Technologys-Impact-on-Library-Services.pdf. DOI: 10.4018/978-1-7998-1482-5.ch002

Innovative technologies for libraries (2022). https://princh.com/blog-8-technologies-to-implement-at-the-library-of-the-future/#.YgY2W99ByUk

Krubu, Dorcas Ejemeh, & Osawaru, Kingsley Efe (2011). The impact of Information and Communication Technology (ICT) in Nigerian University Libraries. *Library Philosophy and Practice (e-journal),* Paper no. 583. https://digitalcommons.unl.edu/libphilprac/583

Mies, Ginny (2016). Use of big data in libraries. http://publiclibrariesonline.org/ 2016/05/using-big-data-to-address-local-needs/

Princh (2018). Current technology trends in libraries. https://princh.com/current-technology-trends-in-libraries/#.XF5W9VwzaUk.

Pujar, Shamprasad M., & Satyanarayana, K.V. (2015). Internet of Things and libraries. *Annals of Library and Information Studies*, 62(Sep.), 186-190.

Shailender Kumar, Sanaman, Gareema, & Rai, Namrata (2008). Federated search: New option for libraries in the digital era. In 6th International CALIBER from February 28-29 & March 1, 2008. University of Allahabad. Ahmedabad, AB: INFLIBNET Centre, 267-285.

Techopedia (2022). Cutting-Edge technologies. https://cutting-edgetechnology/

Waljat (2018). Cloud computing. https://www.waljatcollege.edu.om/downloads.php

2

Challenges in Promotion of E-Learning During COVID-19 Pandemic in India

Sonia Sharma and Piyali Sarkar

Department of Education Lovely Professional University Phagwara, Punjab-144 402

ABSTRACT

World is suffering from coronavirus infection since the end of 2019. Corona virus disease spraying rapidly throughout the world from the beginning of 2020, for that cause it is declared as pandemic by WHO in march 2020. As no proper remedy found for this particular new disease till the date it is become oblivious to maintain social distancing and lock down. Due to the situation each and every sector including the education system totally stopped from March 2020. But we have to maintain the flow of education. Many of the educational institution of India promoted e learning for their students. To avoid coronavirus infection social contact as well as to carry out classes in regular manner, it is become necessary to promote e learning everywhere. But in India the situation is different because Steel we are a poor country where a good number of people do not have a smart phone even. There are many challenges in promotion of e-Learning during this coronavirus pandemic situation in India. In present paper we are going to discuss about some challenges in promotion of e-learning due to coronavirus pandemic situation.

Keywords: e-learning, pandemic, challenges in education.

1. Introduction

Discovery of technology is one of the best things discovered in the history of human civilization. Advancement of technology is reaching to the sky height nowadays. Use of technology is becoming inevitable in every sector of human utility. Show the emergence of educational technology also happened in course of time to make education system more advanced. Main aim of educational technology is to reach the ultimate aim of education all round development by the help of technology. E learning is the concept where teaching learning takes place by the help of internet that is with the help of a online platform. E learning was an emerging topic of recent past in Indian education sector. Though some private schools were adopted e learning process priory most of the schools of India even can't thought about the implementation of e-learning. India is a village-based country, where till date a good number of people cannot afford to buy a Smartphone, show the imagination of implementation of e-classes are not so trustworthy. But this picture is changing rapidly from the beginning of 2020 as the serious situation occurred due to coronavirus out break or covid-19. From the last of the week of March Indian government declared complete lockdown to maintain the social distancing among peoples and to break the chain of viral infection. Now, the infection of virus has spreading rapidly throughout the country. But the dynamic process of education cannot be stopped due to any kind of disruption. So to maintain to retain the progression of education most of the institutions decided to promote e classes for their students. But we have to keep in mind nothing can be perfect within one day or one month and especially when it comes to the point of education it may take too long time to adopt with new technology-based e classes.

This lockdown situation caused many educational institutions to cancel their regular classes, examinations internship conferences etc. It is becoming very difficult to cope up with the present situation because it caused total closure of all educational institutes suddenly at a time.

2. E-Learning

When learning occurs on the basis of ideal teaching methods and contents along with the help of electronic resources, the process is called e-learning. Teaching learning paradigm and dynamics at changing rapidly. To make the process of teaching learning more interesting and trust vote the sensible and realistic the emergence of use of technology in learning occurred and forwarded as e-learning nowadays.There are many kinds of e-Learning procedures discovered by different scientists they can be broadly classified into following categories:

a) Computer Managed Learning

In computer managed learning system management of system takes place with the help of computer. So, computer acts as a record keeping device mainly. Here, computer is not needed for any kind of direct instructional purposes.

b) Computer Assisted Learning

When learning is totally conducted with the help of computer then the process is called computer assistant learning or CAL. Physical presence of human being as an instructor of class totally not needed here.

c) Synchronous Online Learning

When learning is conducted through video conferencing, online chat, video call etc. or with all potential support by learning communities, the process is called synchronous e-learning. Here learners get more opportunities to solve their queries in real time manner and can immediately get answers from instructors.

d) Asynchronous Online Learning

In asynchronous e learning method, email, support work, discussion boards etc. are used to conduct the whole learning procedure where proper introduction needs more time than synchronous one.

e) Fixed e-Learning

In fixed e-learning system, the e-contents of curriculum are always previously designed and pre-loaded. So, no changes can be made during learning process.

f) Adaptive e-learning

In adaptive e-learning method, according to the need of students or as per the learning style for priorities of student resources are designed, created and delivered.

g) Linear e-learning

Linear type of e-learning includes passage of information between computers and humans, no two ways communication occurs in this type of e-learning system.

h) Interactive Online Learning

In interactive online learning method, two ways communication between students and teachers via computer occurs. It is one of the best examples of problem-solving techniques amongst all e-learning methods.

i) Individual Online Learning

To meet the demand or need of individual student, this kind of individual online learning method developed. No community sense building or group activities can be done here. To meet the expectation of individual learner's learning motto, this technique evolved.

j) Collaborative Online Learning

Collaborative online learning method includes a huge platform where multiple students can gain knowledge and can learn and meet their learning objectives together as a peer group. Community building sense and group activities can be solved easily by this technique.

3. Review of Literature

Swann (1992) , CAI for English as a foreign language, computer & education, It is necessary to better understand why teachers persist with digital technologies, even when local conditions in a school are not ideal. A theory normally applied to business contexts, continuance theory, might be useful here. Continuance theory– different from the "Technology Adoption Model" used to inform the Chilean study by Aldunate and Nussbaum (2013).

Sassen (2002) discovered that e learning has an effect on culture. It has a positive affinity with new generation it has a Deep impact among new generation because of its dynamicity and other consequences on the social activities. The acceptance of e-Learning is very much shown among young people because its pattern of quick spreading of consequences, accessibility throughout the world etc. He also mentioned that e learning is the cause of erosion of cultural values among youth in Africa.

Anderson (2008), identified different areas of difficulty in implementation of e-learning, in a case study conducted in Sri Lanka. 1887 respondents including students and University staff involved in data collection from the year 2004 to 2007. This study identified seven major areas and challenges such as: support by students, flexibility of the course, teaching-learning activities, access to internet, confidence of the students and teacher both, localization of setup and attitude towards e-learning. Research on concluded that these factors are concerned with individual development of a student. If proper concerns can be given with the previous factors, the implementation and attitude towards e-learning will be improved gradually.

Mapuva (2009) mentioned 4 issues that can evoke in promotion of e-learning, i.e., institutional leadership, training of teaching staff for adequate infrastructural backup, change in structure of organization, formation of helpful learning ambience. Along with these four factors researcher inferred that student are needed to be mentally prepared for adaptation of e-learning, educational understanding of the students, flexibilities for time, management of time, feasibility etc. are the most important challenges for promotion of e-learning.

Clarke (2015) depicted those Massive open online courses (MOOCs) have taken great position after 2008 in global scenario in the field of education. In his analytical and insightful study, he shown that it plays a great role in advancement of learning procedure and obviously it comes under e-learning category he also mentioned that MOOCs have tremendous potential for social implementation in higher education sector for both developed and developing countries.

Njenga (2018) discover that socio cultural aspects are one of the majors contribute in events in acceptance and effectiveness of e learning. Cultural identity, globalizations, westernization, foreign ideology etc. are the chief regulator of implementation of e-Learning and acceptance of it.

Mishra *et al.* (2020) conducted an online survey wheat 716 trainees of ophthalmology course throughout the India by various social networking platforms. Their study also included some of research fellows in ophthalmology division they found almost 80% trainees felt that CoVID-19 lockdown had a negative impact in their surgical training 55% reported which there increase in stress level due to covid-19 lockdown situation. Almost 76% student responded that the online classes and winners where very useful for them but 77% students admitted that covid-19 lockdown adversely affected in their learning also some of them are preparing virtual classes and simulation-based training permanently.

Jena (2020) worked on effect of covid-19 over the students of open and distance learning course of Indira Gandhi National open University and concluded that covid-19 situation has created many challenges as well as opportunities for the educational institutions to strengthen their technological infrastructure. He recommended that government and non-government stakeholders should also adopt the policy of providing online education, free internet and free digital gadgets to all learners in order to encourage them and utilize their time through online educational opportunities.

Kapasia *et al.* (2020) conducted a online survey with Google forms. Days and q lizards the forms through WhatsApp and email and gathered to 32 students response of college and university level of West Bengal. They found an interesting result that 70% of the whole population is regularly involved with classes through their Android phones. They reported that students are facing various problems due to their classes and found depression, anxiety, unfavorable environment for study, interrupted of no internet connectivity etc among them due to e-classes. The recommended are resilient education system that can ensure that the development of skills for employability and productivity among the students.

Kumar (2020) depicted some remedies to avoid the stress causing due to lock down situation and e classes. According to him, promotion of digital open book, online examination system, interactive virtual environment etc. are the ways to overcome stress among students. Raju (2020) recommended employing an innovative teaching technique for e-learning to overcome stress and anxiety growth among the students.

4. Global Acceptance of E-Learning

Globalization of e-learning happened in early 2000s. Most of the developed countries like USA, Japan *etc*. uses e-learning method as their regular pedagogical method. USA Government education policy includes enormous emphasis on e learning. Globalization of e-Learning refers to the political and cultural also economical integrity among all countries. Globalizations are all sorts of implementations like reduction in in house wise income, introduction of fees per student, growth of tourism in international sector even by cutting public sector budget etc. It is a kind of find mixing of technology and advancement of education system.

Clegg *et al*. 2003 mentioned that the rapid growth of e-Learning system throat inter UK causes a good impact throughout the country as it become available to each and every pupil situated in each part of country. Side by side the fees of the costing regarding that very study and the supplies for the requirements for the same increased a lot also. It is creating unwanted pressure among students and their parents.

One of the most important key determining factors of globalization are taken to be visualized by the dynamics of technological innovation and capitalistic expansion coupled with the decline of nation state as a locus of power. Many scientists found that ICT has devastating effect on globalization of education in field of e learning. ICT makes educational virtual platform easier to access it creates and easy virtual learning environment. It was found that the computing capacity among people increased rapidly in an exponential rate which is very impressive sounding. This is another cause of development of new technologies and advancement of different applications nowadays (Clegg, 2011). It is grown very distinguishingly that as the process will be more virtual it will become more real. Presently due to covid-19 situation many of the institutes have already employed their own virtual learning management system (LMS) as an extension of e-learning system.

Njenga (2018) discover that socio cultural aspects are one of the majors contribute in events in acceptance and effectiveness of e learning. This study is confined in Africa. It was also revealed by this paper that implementation of e learning in higher education in Africa is in a very progressive rate because there are too many barriers regarding implementation of e learning the acceptance rate for the same is very high because of technology prone ness among common people. He also said that ICT please a key role regarding the acceptance and socio-cultural aspects of e-learning.

Many IT companies which deal with software and hardware businesses are developing new applications day by day for the promotion and implementation of e-learning this is growing in a very rapid rate. This is another cause for globalization of e-learning in education. They also mentioned that ICT is playing another key role in rapid development of e-learning globally.

In a Thai case study by Pagram and Pagram (2006) reveals that local people were very affectionate towards using technology in their education but they have accepted it as a side mode of education not so solely deliverable system of education. Culturally it has a negative impact among the people. Also, it was revealed that the interface design software used and planning was very poor in comparison to other countries at that moment. Use of animations and required graphics were lacking also.

5. Challenges of E-Learning

A. There are some benefits found of e-learning, which are as follows

- **Promotion Digital literacy:** e-Learning can be the way out for promoting digital literacy in third world country like India. Economically developed countries have already introduced digital learning facilities for their students but in India there was a lag in promoting digital learning which could be done now by promoting e-classes.
- **Implementation of Blended Learning:** From the very first beginning of 21st century economically developed countries introduced blended learning as their way of teaching to make learning more interesting for their children. In this covid-19 situation implementation of blended learning also possible by promoting e learning.
- **Rise of Learning Management System:** Learning management system is another fruits of knowledge tree developed by human civilization. In case of e learning management systems are used heavily by other countries. Learning management system can save time and pace of study. So it is another good aspect of e-learning.
- **Increase soft copy of learning materials for study:** In India most of the students and very much used to with pen and paper method of study they always takes note through pen and paper and always uses the same for their study. Use of soft copy of learning material can be increased by the help of e learning.
- **Online meeting:** Online classes gives opportunity to meet teacher by the help of internet which could be a good way out instead of going school right now to avoid infection.
- **Collaborative learning:** Collaborative learning felicitates peer learning process. Online activities enhance the peer learning process.so it is one of the most important aspects of scientific way of education.

- **Use of internet for study purpose:**Uses of internet for the purpose of study are very much limited in India with the promotion of e learning the internet usage for study will be increased so the good use of internet can be seen by this way
- **Open and Distance Learning:**A few universities in India have introduced open and distance learning mode of education till 2020 which is one of the most important mode of distance learning. This could be amplified through e-learning.
- **Worldwide exposure:**Worldwide exposure could be possible with the help of e learning by the use of tremendous amount of internet
- **Time management:** Time is the most valuable thing in student life. So time management is one of the most matters of concern. Will time management can be done by e learning mode.
- **Expansion of knowledge:** Knowledge could be amplified and up to date during classroom studies by the use of internet.
- **Promotion of Technology based education:** Introduction of technology driven classroom will be done by this method.
- **Technological advancement:** Advancement of Technology happening rapidly along with the progression of civilization. It is also very important to accept and use the technological progression in regular classroom so it is very important to introduce e learning in form of regular classes.

B. Some disadvantages of promoting e-learning are also noticed, which are given as follows

- **Employment crisis:** Promotions of e-classes may rise the crisis in employment. In India a large number of educated youths always dreams for getting job in education sector promotion of e-classes may reduce the chance of their getting jobs earlier.
- **Lack of adequately trained teachers:** For smooth conduction of e classes, Proper teachers training for ICT driven classes are need of the hour. There is an utmost need of properly trained teachers which is lacking very much in present condition.
- **Deficit of interaction with teachers:** In e learning mode there exists a huge deficiency in face-to-face interaction between pupil and teachers, which could not be filled by any other process.
- **Increase responsibility among parents to educate their child:** With progression of e classes the responsibility of parents gradually increases

because to complete the tasks given in classes or to complete the assignments or giving exam online total responsibility shifted from teachers to every parent.

- **Difficulties in decision making:** Face to face interaction always helps her child to take any kind of decision instantly which is tremendously lacking in e-classes
- **Unpreparedness of teacher student both:** e-learning includes strategic policy making to conduct a smooth e-class. Due to unpreparedness of both students and teachers the quality of e classes decreases.
- **Lack of proficiency among educators and students both about the technique:** Technology competence is the best thing in e-learning but unpracticed and unskilled people can ruin the essence of e-classes. As in Indian education system we are not very much used to with e-classes the chances of ruining the class exists highly.
- **Curriculum development:** Relevant content design and curriculum development is utmost need of the hour. Development of which needs good amount of time, effort and knowledge. So, relevance centric curriculum development is another crisis in present situation.
- **Student centrism:** E-learning course should be more students centric. High pedagogical skills along with technological readiness are needed to create such kind of content. So, this is one of the most important challenge in implementation of e learning in India
- **Flexibility of the course content:** Contents of the e learning curriculum should be flexible and should meet the individual need of each and every student who will access that, which is very tough and challenging job itself.

6. Conclusion

Daily life of each and every individual of this world interrupted due to covid-19 attack. Each and every person in the world is suffering from mental and physical stress economic downfall anxiety and stress. In education system of India, the reflection of anxiety and sterol stress among the students found in through to previous studies. Though e-learning environment comes with some barriers it has too many positive effects also discussed earlier. So, it is very necessary call of the hour to implement e learning with proper infrastructure and through government policies in each and every institution of India. Spreading positive awareness towards e-learning also needed very much to wipe out the misconceptions and lesser-known facts among the parents and the students.

learning can induce digital literacy worldwide exposure of introvert people expansion of knowledge it could be facilitative for promotion of blended learning and open and distance learning system.

References

Andersson, A. (2008). Seven major challenges for e-learning in developing countries: Case study eBIT, Sri Lanka. *International journal of education and development using ICT*, 4(3), 45-62.

Bates, A. T. (2005). *Technology, e-learning and distance education*. Routledge.

Cantoni, V., Cellario, M., & Porta, M. (2004). Perspectives and challenges in e-learning: towards natural interaction paradigms. *Journal of Visual Languages & Computing*, 15(5), 333-345.

Challenges and Opportunities created by Covid-19 for ODL: A case study of IGNOU. *International Journal for Innovative Research in Multidisciplinary Filed*, Volume-6, Issue- 5, pp. 217-222.

Clarke, T. (2013). The advance of the MOOCs (massive open online courses): The impending globalisation of business education?. *Education+ Training*.

Clegg, S., Hudson, A., & Steel, J. (2003). The emperor's new clothes: Globalisation and e-learning in higher education. *British Journal of Sociology of Education*, 24(1), 39-53.

Crawford, J., Butler-Henderson, K., Rudolph, J., Malkawi, B., Glowatz, M., Burton, R., & Lam, S. (2020). COVID-19: 20 countries' higher education intra-period digital pedagogy responses. *Journal of Applied Learning & Teaching*, 3(1), 1-20.

Dwivedi, Y. K., Hughes, D. L., Coombs, C., Constantiou, I., Duan, Y., Edwards, J. S., & Raman, R. (2020). Impact of COVID-19 pandemic on information management research and practice: Transforming education, work and life. *International Journal of Information Management*, 102211. https://doi.org/10.1016/j.ijinfomgt.2020.102211.

Islam, N., Beer, M., & Slack, F. (2015). E-learning challenges faced by academics in higher education. *Journal of Education and Training Studies*, 3(5), 102-112.

Iyengar, K., Mabrouk, A., Jain, V. K., Venkatesan, A., & Vaishya, R. (2020). Learning opportunities from COVID-19 and future effects on health care system. *Diabetes & Metabolic Syndrome: Clinical Research & Reviews*, 14(5), 943-946.

Jena, P. K. (2020). Impact of pandemic COVID-19 on education in India.

Kapasia, N., Paul, P., Roy, A., Saha, J., Zaveri, A., Mallick, R., & Chouhan, P. (2020). Impact of lockdown on learning status of undergraduate and postgraduate students during COVID-19 pandemic in West Bengal, India. *Children and Youth Services Review*, 116,105194.

Khetrapal, S., & Bhatia, R. (2020). Impact of COVID-19 pandemic on health system & sustainable development goal 3. *Indian Journal of Medical Research*, 151(5), 395.

Kumar, A., Nayar, K. R., &Koya, S. F. (2020). COVID-19: Challenges and its consequences for rural health care in India. *Public Health in Practice*, 100009.

Kumar, D. N. S. (2020). Impact of Covid-19 on Higher Education. *Higher Education Digest*. https://www.highereducationdigest.com/impact-of-covid-19-on-highereducation/

Kwofie, Benjamin, & Henten, Anders (2011). The advantages and challenges of e-learning implementation: The story of a developing nation.

Lau, R. W., Yen, N. Y., Li, F., & Wah, B. (2014). Recent development in multimedia e-learning technologies. *World Wide Web*, *17*(2), 189-198.

Mapuva, J. (2009). Confronting challenges to e-learning in higher education institutions. *International Journal of Education and Development Using ICT*, 5(3), 101-114.

Mishra, D., Nair, A. G., Gandhi, R. A., Gogate, P. J., Mathur, S., Bhushan, P., & Singh, M. K. (2020). The impact of COVID-19 related lockdown on ophthalmology training programs in India–Outcomes of a survey. *Indian Journal of Ophthalmology*, 68(6), 999.

Nagy, A. (2005). The impact of e-learning. In *E-Content* (pp. 79-96). Springer, Berlin, Heidelberg.

Nicola, M., Alsafi, Z., Sohrabi, C., Kerwan, A., Al-Jabir, A., Iosifidis, C., & Agha, R. (2020). The socio-economic implications of the coronavirus pandemic (COVID-19): A review. *International Journal of Surgery* (London, England), 78, 185.

Njenga, J. K. (2018). Sociocultural paradoxes and issues in e-learning use in higher education Africa. *Globalisation, Societies and Education*, 16(1), 120-133.

Pagram, P., &Pagram, J. (2006). Issues in ELearning: A thai case study. *The Electronic Journal of Information Systems in Developing Countries*, 26(1), 1-8.

Raju, H. (2020).Covid-19 Lockdown-Challenges To Higher Education, Dr. AIT, ECE, Bengaluru, (ongoing project).20944/preprints202004.02oi:10.20944/

Sassen, Saskia. 2002. Towards a Sociology of Information Technology. *Current Sociology*, 50 (3), 365–388. doi:10. 1177/0011392102050003005.

Singh, M. K., & Neog, Y. (2020). Contagion effect of COVID19 outbreak: Another recipe for disaster on Indian economy. *Journal of Public Affairs*, e2171.

Uhomoibhi, J., & Ross, M. (2013, June). Globalisation and e-learning: integrating university and professional qualifications for employability and lifelong learning. In *Proceedings of the 8th Internatýonal Conference on E-Learning. Book Series: Proceedings of the International Conference on e-Learning* (pp. 404-408).

Verma, A., & Prakash, S. (2020). Impact of covid-19 on environment and society. *Journal of Global Biosciences*, 9(5),7352-7363.

WHO, 2020. WHO Director-General's Opening Remarks at the Media Briefing on COVID- Retrieved from. https://www.who.int/dg/speeches/detail/who-directorgeneral-s-opening-remarks-at-the-media-briefing-on-covid-19-11-march-2020.

3

Designing Users Friendly Mobile Library Apps: An Overview

Sudip Bhattacharjee

Department of Library and Information Science
Maharaja Bir Bikram University, Agartala, Tripura -799 001

ABSTRACT

With the advancement of mobile technology, the usage of mobile application has increased significantly which leads to change the life style of common people. Library is also not an exception in this context. Library and Information Science Professionals have started to incorporate the changes from the beginning of ICT advancement with an idea "library should be within thumb of people". Mobile application plays vital role to fulfil the objective of library. Most of the library has started or planning to start the service to its user with various services effectively. But, the process to provide library service through mobile application is not satisfactory till date. No too much usage of libraries mobile apps can be seen; even which mobile applications are in use, most of them are almost inactive form.

But the various recent surveys show us the tremendous growth of the usage of mobile application among people. According to Google, (2017) the user survey shows that mobile can fast-track time to purchase by 20% through facilitating efficiencies in decision-making and enhanced team collaboration, particularly with more complex purchases. On this ground, an attempt is taken to understand the needs and recent development of library services with advance Library Mobile Apps. Further, this study will help us to understand the various issues and aspects of Library Mobile Apps. This, study also gives us an idea about how to create best Library Mobile Apps by considering various parameters such as appearance, usages, friendly looks and others important features for our library users.

Keywords: Mobile Application, Library Service, Apps Service, Mobile Apps.

1. Introduction

With the changing and dynamic role of Information Communication Technology, the Library and Information Professional faces various challenges to become up to date with the challenges. Soon after introduction of mobile technology into the mankind, the prospective of people changes dynamically for getting the best services with user friendly or smart technology. Mobile App is an example of it. A mobile applications, is also known as mobile app, which is nothing but an application software designed to run on a mobile device. Mobile applications provide serve to the users almost similar to the computer technology. But, the applications are generally minimize in size, individual software units with multiple functions. From children to adults, we are now installing and finding information with the mobile app. According to an American monetization company report, people now spend two hours for using apps in a day. So, 86% of mobile user's time is spent using mobile apps. Thus, mobile apps are everywhere, and their number is increasing day by day.

At the same time, libraries also planning to develop mobile library apps for its users to provide the best service. The 2014 NMC Horizon Report (library edition) identifies mobile apps as an important development in technology for academic libraries. It also identifies as a key challenge the task of rethinking the role and skills of academic librarians. (1) In the higher education edition of the same report, the shift from students as consumers to students as creators is identified as a key trend. (2) Also in 2014, the American Library Association announced that it supports makerspaces in libraries. (3) The makerspace movement encompasses not only 3-D printing, but all kinds of content creation—everything from supporting local writers to offering digital media labs for creating multimedia content. Libraries are becoming more integrated into their communities by offering services like these.

2. Why We Need Mobile App for Library?

Library users are generally those people who are seeking some kinds of information of their own. They generally seek information for their day to day information seeking. Due to advancement of mobile technology, the people practically in India start frequently uses of this technology.

In a latest survey, it is believed that almost 75% people of India will use mobile phone by 2030. This brings a great opportunity for the library to get library user's attention. Mobile application allows libraries to connect with patrons and also feel patron's new types of refresh service. It can provide a wide array of library services to its users as shown below.

- ***Access and View of Library Account:*** Like other apps, using a mobile app within library, library users can check due dates, renew book, place hold, and get new alerts.
- ***Book Identification:*** Library users also can locate and find branch location of book within shelves and its availability.

- ***Browsing of Database:*** It provides access to a variety of library resources and database. Thus, library users can enter any search terms and view results that are designed specifically for mobile viewing. This types of service includes OPAC service, Web-OPAC service, integrated search, and document search, etc.
- ***Catalogue Search:*** Library users can search the catalogue by author, subject, ISBN, title, publisher, keyword, etc. They can also view the softcopy of cover images, book review, and more.
- ***Notification Alerts:*** Library users get various kinds of alerts services on news, notices, events through SMS or MMS wherever there is a events. They also have a provision to select the choice of types of service they need.
- ***Reference service:*** Library users can get reply of their inquiries regarding any facts or service information by providing instant answers, with possible hyperlinks to articles/references in shortest time.
- ***Referral service:*** Library users also can get reply of their inquiries if document are not even available within the library by providing hyperlinks or reference of the link to articles/references for nearest library.

3. Types of Mobile Apps

According to Mishra (2017), mobile apps can be broadly categorised into three categories as discussed below:

- Native App
- Web App
- Hybrid App

Native App: Native applications refer to applications that are specifically written and developed for a specific mobile operating system. In order to create true, native applications, the Java programming language must be used for Android, the Objective C programming language for iOS, and the .NET framework for Windows Phone.

Web App: Web app refers to for mobile versions of websites. It runs by a browser and typically written in HTML5. Web apps became really popular when HTML5 came around and people realized that they can obtain native-like functionality in the browser. Social Media site face book web application example of such type of app.

Hybrid App: A hybrid web app is an application that is neither truly a mobile web app nor a native app. Hybrid apps are a way to expose content from existing Web sites in app format. It is basically an application written with the aforementioned web techniques of HTML5, JavaScript APIs, and CSS, but it runs inside a 3rd party native app container. Some of the well-known and used hybrid mobile frameworks are PhoneGap, Appcelerator, and Appspresso. (Mishra, 2017)

4. Mobile Apps: Features

There are various kinds of Mobile Applications which are continually added to web day by day to provide best service. Marketers are also experimenting with their own app experiences process. It is also found that the investment of mobile application is around $3 billion on app install advertising in 2015, an increase of 80% from 2014; which shows massive shift in consumer behaviour. It's become very problematic for apps developers to get people and to meet the need of the app users comfortably for downloading the apps successfully for long time. As most of the apps users (almost 25%) open an application once and if they feel unhappy, never return back to it.

Jenny Gove, UX Research Lead, Google describe the various feature of Apps into six main categories such as app exploration, apps navigation, app search, usability and comprehension. Similarly we can incorporate the feature at Library Mobile Apps.

5. Factors Incorporate Before the Development of Library Apps

We can reveal the points mentioned by Gove while explaining the categories and feature of Mobile Apps into Mobile Library Apps, as mentioned below.

- **Show the value of app at upfront:** The library users should be able to engage by addressing tasks clearly at front and center location. The features such as OPAC, Circulation Disk, Important Events, etc. should be highlighted at front place. The frequent experiment also leads to create frustration and confusion among users.
- **Organize and label Menu and Sub-Menu user-friendly:** Library users most of the time struggle to interpret menu and sub-menu as the library terms such as OPAC, Referral Tool, etc. are not commonly known to the users. So, Menu should be categories such a way which should be clear from user's prospects with no overlapping.
- **By "Go back" easily**: Most of the time users want to go back behind the steps. Application should leverage back functionality and very easily, so that users don't feel problematic to get into it or to start over again from the home screen.

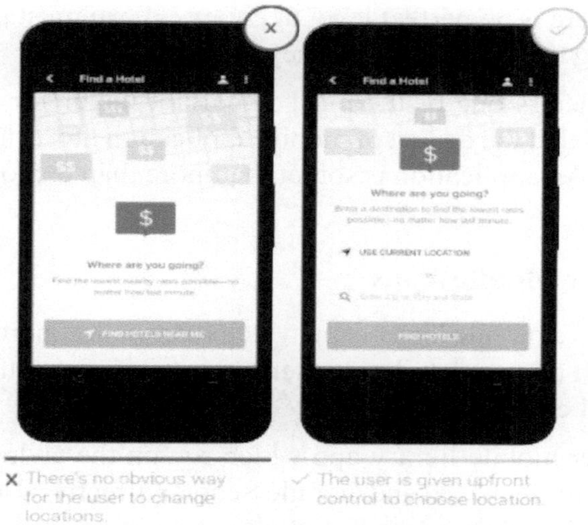

(*Source:* https://www.thinkwithgoogle.com/marketing-resources/experience-design/chapter-1-app-navigation-and-exploration/ Page.7)

- **Auto-detection of location**: This is most vital feature for library apps. If we can create library apps such a way that it can locate the book items from shelves, this will solve the problem of accessing material in least possible time.
- **Friendly Access among mobile apps and web:** Library users sometime get confused or frustrated when an app and web of the same looks and feel differently in layout. It is also a good idea to make similar looks and layout as much as possible for both web and apps.
- **Prominently display the search field:** Library users mostly will look for specific search of an item. They often prefer to go for browsing. Apps that do not have a prominently placed search box at from beginning page can cause user frustration and slow the user down.
- **Retrieval Result of Information:** It must be ensure that search results are useful. If possible library apps should provide search display with artificial intelligence. These tools can reduce the likelihood of user errors. They will also help speed up the search process and keep users on-task toward conversion.
- **Easy Password Authentication Process:** Users most of the time get annoyed, when they have to go through an arduous or multi-step task to set up or reset a password. Reduce the risk of abandonment by simplifying the authentication experience during login.
- **Control the level of Zoom:** Users most of the time also wants to be able to control the level of zoom when they view an image or document. They

can become frustrated if there is no perfect level of zoom. So, we must put users in control by allowing user to zoom in as they prefer.

Moreover, a good User Interface is one of the most important factor for an app's success. Steve Jobs stated that the design of mobile application more than just the looks like or feels like. An application is something more than the look with a good design.

6. Examples of Some Library Mobile Apps

LibAnywhere: LibAnywhere is a mobile library app which runs on the android phone and other iOS devices. It allows the library users to access information such as catalogues, events, and contact details.

Redcube: ReadCube is another mobile library app which run on the android phone. ReadCube users can search PubMed and Google Scholar directly. Users can also make notes on pdf by directly editing, and also get option on later search.

Endnote: EndNote is also a library app, which is subscribed by reference management tool and developed by Thomson Reuters. It provides analysis and manage the citations pattern based on web based and desktop program.

E-Resource Publisher App: The E-Resource Publisher App is a mobile library app based to provide service to the library users. It provides full time access to e-resources. Library users easily can download the full-text as they needs.

ScienceDirect: The ScienceDirect Mobile application is another mobile apps service which is provided by Elsevier. It contents SciVerse, ScienceDirect for Apple and Android mobile application.

ACS Journals: ACS Mobile application service is provided by the American Chemical Society. ACS Mobile service can be accessed from Apple or Android platform. It provides full-text access of the document.

Some other publisher like: Springer provide Mobile app service such as Springerlink, Aggregator Ebsco provide Mobile app service such as EbscoHost to share the universe of knowledge.

7. Conclusion

Mobile Apps are the needs of the hour. Though there are various kindly of mobile library apps are available for us; but it is yet to be popular. Mobile apps allow libraries to connect with users by feel user a refresh and new service. Thus, library and information Science must take the necessary steps to make apps more convenient for library users so that both the librarians and the users can be benefit from it. There is also need to proper marketing of the mobile apps service among the users community, library should take the proper steps in this regards.

References

Glassman, N.R. (2012). The mobile medical library: Is there an app for that? *Journal of Electronic Resources in Medical Libraries*, 9(2), 147-154.

https://www.apteligent.com/wp-content/uploads/2016/07/PRINCIPLES-MOBILE-APP-DESIGN-WP.pdf (Accessed on 21/08/2021)

https://www.inflibnet.ac.in/caliber2009/CaliberPDF/33.pdf (Accessed on 21/08/2021)

https://www.moveoapps.com/ultimate-guide-to-mobile-app-design-principles (Accessed on 21/08/2021)

https://www.thinkwithgoogle.com/marketing-resources/experience-design/principles-of-mobile-app-design-introduction/ (Accessed on 21/08/2021)

https://www.thinkwithgoogle.com/marketing-resources/experience-design/chapter-1-app-navigation-and-exploration/ (Accessed on 21/08/2021)

https://www.youtube.com/watch?v=e1uqSy_0hmY

Khare, Nidhi (2012). Libraries on move: Library mobile applications. 7th International CALIBER-2009, 272.

Zhu, W., Marquez, A., & Yoo, J. (2015). Engineering economics jeopardy! Mobile app for university students. *The Engineering Economist*, 60, 291-306.

4

Information Economy and the Role of Library in Digital Era

Jitamoni Bhattacharyya[1] and Bandana Gogoi[2]

Librarian , Biswanath College of Agriculture, Assam-784176

[2]Department of History, Biswanath College of Agriculture, Assam-784176

ABSTRACT

The chapter focuses that information as an economic resources and the role of library to distributing information among the user's communities. From the economic point of view-the most important properties of information are easy to access and limited money acquire more information i.e. cost benefit. Information economy makes people ware about their goal and library help people to provide resources on need base.

Keyword: Information economy, Library, Information Communication Technology, ICT, Users' community.

1. Introduction

Library is considered as main gate of knowledge creation and dissemination among user communities. The main role of the library is to collect information in all aspects. In relation to history library plays a major role to collect past events information and preserved for future. Therefore it can be mentioned that it effect in the growth of Indian economy. With the help of information various decisions will be taken which help in the growth of economy and able to compare the price of goods and others. In this context role of library is vary essential for preparing different activities, take decision mainly in marketing sector which has effect in economic growth. For that:

- Decision maker can adopt suitable policy for increase the rate of economic growth.
- Able to compare past and present situation
- Know about the more demandable product and adopt necessary steps.

- Scientist can point out the most drawbar of economic growth and adopted different strategy to dissolve it.
- Policy maker can prepare sweet able policy to improve the economic condition from time to time.
- In relation to information economy and library we mention here four models such as:
    - Collection status of the library.
    - Library consider as a centre of resource sharing
    - Services of the library embedded
    - Consider as a access of knowledge/information

In this digital era help people to meet the changing needs of the society by the help of information dissemination and empowered them to go ahead.

- We visited to the library the library run after us.
- Collection of the library-there is no wall
- Information spread in right time. It means able to acquire recent information's...What is going on in day to day life?

Information economy makes people aware about their goods. And people able to compare the goods in price rate. In this 21st century library users demand that information in –time (current information) means information help them and aware them about what is going on and it effect in socio-economic development. User can find out the answer of the specific question and adopt strategy to solve the problem. Now people want knowledge based economy, mass people search where the law cost and good quality material are found. In this regards information economy filled up the user's needs. Mainly in business sector information economy has great impact. There should be a balance between economy and goods. Library adopted many techniques for solving the issues mainly:

- Cost benefit
- Save the time
- Fast information
- Society depend on information and information depend on society
- Development of information communication technology(ICT)
- Information exploration per second and the role of library to manage them by the use of different digital devices.

Information society is known as knowledge created society. Early literacy services are contributing to long term economic success mainly depends upon on document which is preserved by the library. There is a co-relation between economic development and investment in early literacy. It impact on long term economic development.

2. Public Library is a Catalyst-for Increase the Growth rate of Economy

Mainly public library disseminates the ideas/knowledge/information among the people with a goal to develop their mindset/create knowledge in different field. There is no restriction among the user. Every person of the society can take their opportunity to collect the material on need base without any barrier. It can be mentioned that public library plays a crucial role indirectly in the growth of economic rate.

3. Public Library as a Power for Resources

Public library are mentioned as a power of resources where user can able to get their material. The main aim of public library is to collect material, repository and disseminate among the user community.

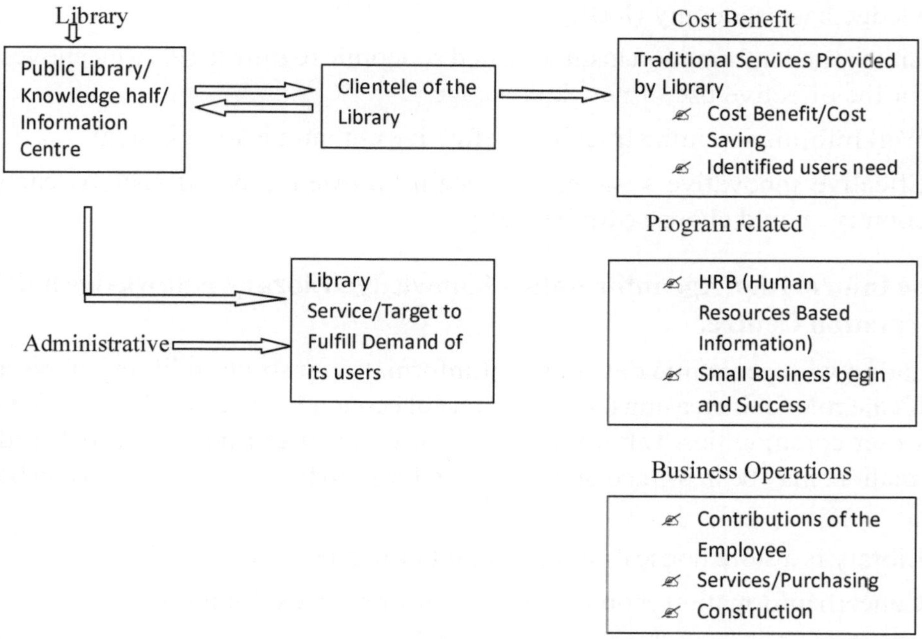

Figure: Model Showed the Economic Benefited From Library

3.1. Workforce Skill

Library always trying to increased work force skill among the library workers.

3.2. Business Support

Support to increase the small business by providing recent information.

3.3. Strong Collection

Know better the user/understand user's need.

4. Knowledge Based Economy

Some points of knowledge based economy are mentioned below:

- Knowledge input measuring
- Knowledge preserved and dissemination
- Knowledge flow
- Out-put knowledge measuring
- Networking system measuring

The World Bank adopted the methodology for knowledge assessment and score cards. There are 64 variable and consider them important for development of knowledge base economy (KBE).

- Library and information institution and economic regime to serve incentives for the effective use of new knowledge.
- Well Information infrastructure to effective communication system.
- Effective innovative system. To sustain knowledge based society, each country should choose own best way.

5. The Information Age/information Knowledge/Library/Knowledge half/ Information Centre.

In relating with economic development information institution/library plays a significant role for increasing the growth rate of economy by serving best services to its user communities. Library is one point where user find out value based information, may be in printed or non printed form. In this point of view it can be said:

- Library is a store house of information/knowledge
- Concern information economy where information exploration rapidly
- Library reduces the bridge gap of information exploration and users of information
- Aware people to take right decision at right time as we live in democratic society
- Different type of collection helps people to find out their material

It has been seen that many changes in this era due to globalization. Artificial intelligence takes place and information forms within a second. Many terms are used to identify the actual changing the society such as:

- Industrial Society
- Global Village
- Knowledge based Society, *etc.*

Information economy is a part of micro-economic theory. Information system (IS) which effect in our social life, and growth of economic development and decision making.

6. Characteristics of Information

Information has many characteristics such as:

- Information spread very fast but difficult to accept all because of many fails information spread among them
- Information assists to take right decision in every field
- Effect on socio-economic development.

So information is the key factor where decision will be taken on the basis of the information and prepare many effective planes which increased the rate of economic growth.

Economics is a multidisciplinary area includes all activities of people in context to day by day life- like working life style, healthy mind and healthy body. Information economy focuses various areas such as:

- Medicine and health care
- Changing Environment
- Collaboration Internationally
- Focus an economic growth
- Agricultural sector/Farming
- Others-it includes cost for transportation. Importance for personal mobility in the knowledgeable society, designing for disability people, *etc.*

7. Impact of Information Communication Technology in Knowledge Transfer

By the used of Internet information technology make it possible to see the world and actual picture what is happening and what will be take for future plane. Download information from any part of the world and store it. Introduce of World Wide Web (www), all are possible in all places. Most powerfull in

USA. Information delivery system by the use of radio, computer, and television, and newspaper, *etc.* people can learn and gain knowledge.

Technology can change rapidly the way of information is accessed and disseminated. In this regards library adopt many strategy so that information collect and spread among the society. Also adopt new technology for better services and make traditional to modern with the help of electronic devices. By politically, great importance has been paid to make society to information society with the help of different globalization like:

- UNO
- World Bank
- International telecommunication unit (ITU), which is based on Information Communication Technology.

The dynamic and frequently development of ICT having interlink between different countries of the world and it has great impact in socio-economic development, increased the growth rate of economy. Here mentioned some point which effect to the economic development.

- Government given more attention in the development of ICT world wise
- Electronic devices, which are different country wise, can use ICT for increased the growth rate of economy
- Mainly developed and developing country trace more attention to increase the economic condition by the use of ICT in different activities and trying to making project in different field.

Library and information centre environment is now a day's undergoing a rapid change and dynamic evolution. Applying various electronic devices, on line text, hypertext etc. library can able to information processing and distributing. Library can open E-Mail, Fax, *etc.* to facilitate the DDS (Document Delivery System).

8. Future benefits

Prime Minister of India is trying to make India a Global Information Technology supreme power. So Government of India took many strategies for introducing National Task Force on information technology and software development. Some major point highlight here:

- Set up Internet Gateway access to disseminate information
- On IT software, there is no customs and excise duty it means zero
- Also income tax exemption. No tax regarding software export
- Encourage private company to prepared software in different activities

- Importance to networking among various universities/research institutes
- Offer financial package for purchasing computers.
- Sweat Equity
- Assist to prepared multidisciplinary project in development in IT sector
- Improve the quality of services and improve man power quality and skills.

Today's people are different from the people of yesterday because of rapidly change of ICT. Information communication technology has great effect in now a day's society where information exploration very fast. More and more information stored and exploration per second. We are living in the digital era where society is highly knowledgeable and self conscious i.e. modern society. Life style of people change and demand of goods increased day by day and services. Society expects more information. Because of that, the rate of literacy is increased.

Academic institution used computer and ICT for teaching learning process; In fact today's people are better informed and can contract each other without any boundary.

9. Conclusion

Information economy has great impact in the economic growth and library plays a crucial role in upgrade literacy rate. Library can manage the whole system and serve quick services to its users communities. In 21st century information is the basic factor where Social welfare, primary economy are the production, preserved and dissemination of information.

References

Dutta, R., & Sundharas, M. (2005). Indian economy. New Delhi: S. Chand & Company.

Ramaiah, L.S. *et al.* (1997). Information and society. New Dehli: Ess Ess Publications, pp 31-32.

https://digitalcommonos.edu

https://ejournals.bc.edu

https://web.simmons.edu

https://www.emerald.com

https://www.ripublication.com

5

Competent Library Services in Academic Environment and Total Quality Management (TQM) Practices

Abinash Dash[1] and B. Chandrabati [2]

[1]*Institute of Hotel Management (An Autonomous Body Under Ministry of Tourism Govt. of India) Bhubaneswar, Odisha - 751007*
[2]*MLIS, IGNOU, Bhubaneswar, Odisha - 751013*

ABSTRACT

Academic libraries are unique, essential and strategic hubs inside our social cloth which are advanced primarily based totally at the requirements of the times, to help people in the purchase of good enough facts that could allow them to decorate their information, for the development in their wellness and that of the society at large. To attain their goal, they ought to generate, filter, control and diffuse correct and well timed human information which have been harvested and documented; for the purpose of enriching the highbrow needs in their clients. Like every other kind of library, academic libraries are growing organisms. Justification to the above statement has been captured aptly in the *classic book* of *Ranganathan (1931) entitled 'Five Laws of Library Science'; detailing the principles of the library profession. The* philosophical postulation of Ranganathan's fifth law is a classical position that offers much strength and support for the need to adequately plan for the best strategies to exhibit in academic library environments in order to provide effective services. In other words, *the fore-stated law by Ranganathan has already signaled that academic librarians must be ready at all times* to effectively satisfy the diverse, complex and ever-increasing information needs of their users from the explosive available information resources that spring on a daily basis. As such, addressing this issue would require a holistic management approach by academic libraries that must be internally efficient and externally effective. It is in this context that the question of "total quality management" becomes relevant in the management of academic library environments. While it cannot be out of place to claim that many academic library managers are not practicing the required activities/ management styles that are needed for the purpose of exhibiting satisfactory performance to their teeming population of clienteles, it is appropriate to highlight best strategies through which effective library services can be exhibited in order to increase their relevance, for their continued survival and sustenance in a polarized information landscape.

Keywords: Total Quality Management (TQM), Performance, Strategic planning, Academic environments, Effective library services.

1. Introduction

The Total Quality Management (TQM) method used worldwide for a variety of products and services should also be functional to library services. This helps to get better library services, organize services according to user requirements, ensure quality, maintain quality, and observe from time to time. This will help revalidate library services, ensure that they are good enough to the greater part of library users, meet client needs, and instill self-belief in the library staff that provides these services. As a result, improving library services and supporting on the whole expansion will help the librarian occupation mature, achieve enhanced social status, and meet the expectations of society as a whole.
Libraries are the perfect area to enforce TQM. These are carrier companies devoted to customers, patrons. By developing a strategic plan and adhering to our dedication to non-stop exceptional improvement, library leaders can rework and enhance their organization.

For quite some time before now, the concept of quality has been in existence. Though, its meaning within management landscape has continued to evolve and change over time because prior to the emergence of the TQM concept, the term has undergone some modifications. In the early days, quality was observed and guaranteed by inspection but the approach was developed and modified to become Quality Control, Quality Assurance and more recently, Total Quality management (Munla, 2008). Ever since that time, the theory of quality management has continued to gain a wider acceptance by becoming a management philosophy in its own right, and has taken shape in a series of international standards in the ISO 9000 series Moghaddam and Moballeghi (2008). TQM is the equivalent of what other countries or organizations may call a company-wide quality management system, enterprise quality management system, or integrated quality management system, to name a few (Moghaddam and Moballeghi, 2008).

Dale (1999) defined TQM, in accordance with ISO 8402, "as a management approach of an organization, centered on quality, based on the participation of all its members and aiming at long-term success through customer satisfaction, and benefits to all members of the organization and to society". Donald (2003) as cited by Kumbar (2004) viewed TQM as a systematic process which focuses on understanding customer needs and improving customer services. Similarly, Julnes (2016) sees TQM as an organization-wide, integrative effort to continuously improve the quality of an organization's products or services and fully satisfy the needs and wants of their customers/clients. For Hellsten & Klefsjö ([2000), "TQM is a continuously evolving management system consisting of values, methodologies and tools, the aim of which is to increase external and internal customer satisfaction with a reduced amount of resources" while Barone (2021) sees TQM as the continual process of detecting and reducing or eliminating errors in manufacturing, streamlining supply chain management, improving the customer experience, and ensuring that employees are up to speed with training. From the foregoing definitions, it is clear that TQM is an all-encompassing management strategy whose goal is targeted at customer satisfaction.

2. Principles of Total Quality Management

One of the definitions of a "principle" is that, it is a fundamental truth, law, doctrine, or motivating force, upon which others are based (Collins English Dictionary, n.d.). Principles usually have some major influence on the way things are done. Hence, total quality management principles entails "the complete set of fundamental beliefs, norms, rules and values that are accepted as true and can be used as a basis for total quality management. The TQMPs can be used as a foundation that would guide an organization's performance improvement". The basic principles of total quality as outlined by Dixit (2010) are:

1. **"Focus on the user**: Meeting or exceeding user's needs.
2. **Participation and Teamwork**: Participation through team work to get maximum output.
3. **Employee involvement and Empowerment**: Empowering employees with some authority and responsibility to make them a vital force for achieving quality target.
4. **Continuous Improvement and Learning**: Improvement and learning is never ending process.
5. **Senior Management Commitment**: Librarian must be personally involved in activities such as planning, implementation of policies, reviewing quality performance and interacting with users etc.
6. **Process Identity**: Identifying the process and sub process, interrelating and sequencing them in proper way.
7. **Continuous Process Improvement**:
    - Reduce Resources
    - Reduce Errors

- Meet or exceed the user's requirement
- Make the process safer
- Make the process more satisfying to the person doing

8. **System approach**: Operation should be defined by a system followed by sub System.
9. **Self Assessment**: To know the strength and weakness.
10. **Prevention rather than defecting errors**: By various tools and techniques such as statistical process control.
11. **Strategic planning**: It reveals "who are our users? What are their expectations? How do we achieve this goal? What workforce, machine and money are required? *etc*.
12. **Quality measurement:** "To know what is our current quality level? And what quality level we aspire to achieve?".

On a similar note, Maske and Khiste (2016) outlined total commitment; customer driven services; team management; training; commitment to continuous improvement; empowerment and respecting people; measurement and analysis techniques as the basic components of total quality management.

Based on the principles outlined above, it can be concluded that TQM is a collection of processes. Its purpose is to enable organizations to strive to consistently improve processes by combining the knowledge and experience of their employees to meet customer requirements.

3. Benefits of TQM in Libraries

The goal of any library, regardless of type, is to provide the best possible service to its readers. As a result, a library's success is measured by how well it achieves its goals in terms of its established mission and vision. Interestingly, this cannot be achieved without being best aware of the services provided by users. However, the discovery and application of information and communication technology (ICT) tools in the library field has brought dramatic changes, particularly in academic library practice. Everything to keep you up to date, and a reliable service provider. Kiriri (2018) accurately described the above scenario with the following statement: Agency and Education. For these reasons, Milakovic (2006) emphasized that the way services are delivered at the customer touch point is important for establishing quality control and sustainable improvement. Nonetheless, Miller and Stearns (1994) as cited by LISBDNETWORK (2018) offered the following as some of the benefits that libraries stand to gain if they carefully implement quality management principles:

- "Incremental changes lead to continuous improvement — quick solutions may yield only partial results.
- Forces library managers to develop leadership skills interested of replaying on power within position to obtain results.
- Increase staff participation in decision-making, thus increasing the feeling of "ownership of decisions and directions once charted.
- Improves the level of training given to staff, thus increasing skills.
- Helps break down barriers between library departments and improves communication within the organization.
- Provides a method of improving services to users in a period to similar resources".

The rationale above is not devised from the fact that 21st century academic libraries must apply a strong new governance principle—TQM—in their operations to cope with the economic pressures, structural changes and technological innovations that characterize social realities. According to Musk and Histe (2016), the future of libraries "needs a more user-centric and flexible organizational structure that allows the various components of the library to become more self-managed and adaptable in response to internal and external pressures."

4. Total Quality Management (TQM) Practices for Effective Academic Environments

Globally, all kinds of organizations are realizing the need to practice an all-round management strategy that is tilted towards customer satisfaction. In fact, it has become a key requirement for the sustainability of organizations in as much as they want to remain relevant in a competitive economy. As such, academic libraries cannot be left out in this struggle as they need to provide quality products and services to their clients on a constant basis.

There has been a radical change in many academic libraries in an attempt to keep up with the ever-increasing pool of information in a variety of formats. In libraries, TQM is a comprehensive management strategy that engages all the departments, sections or units of the entire library system. "Many libraries are now creating spaces to promote document and media production as well as technology, group study spaces, and even coffee shops" (Accardi, Cordova, & Leeder, 2010). All of these are in a bid to improve their quality of service via redefining their roles from an emphasis in terms of size of building and collections to a better approach of offering services that are tailored toward the library users' expectations in terms of what counts as quality to the user in a 21st

century environment. For instance, a study conducted by Nitecki & Hernon (2000) on "service quality and customer satisfaction at Yale University's Libraries arrived at the conclusion that service quality and customer satisfaction can be measured from three dimensions namely: tangibles, reliability or service efficiency and affect of service". By implication, library personnel play a major role on the provision of effective library services not only in terms of the resources they provide but in terms of their attitude to their users.

Saur (2007) averred that "libraries have many opportunities to learn from their users in a way that integrates and communicates value across all areas and create an experience where the user feels appreciated as a valued partner, rather than viewing the library as a transaction point for books, material, and information. Further, Saur (2007) argued that rather than marketing, building relationships have proved to better improve the service industry". As such, there is no gainsaying the fact that within academic library environments, the practice of Total Quality Management (TQM) has to come into play as it provides the required tools and direction to improve quality services. This is for the simple reason that academic libraries are by their nature, designed to always take the lead in the provision of high quality information resources and services to their clienteles.

Compared to other types of libraries, academic libraries are known to be proactive in the provision of timely and adequate resources and services in a bid to better serve their patrons. The imperatives of TQM practice has been concretized on the fact that the 21st century has brought about much complexities to the information terrain, leading to a greater demand for the provision of a more effective approach by providing the appropriate information to the right user at right time through the best and easiest medium available.

5. Conclusion

Having a cursory look at the previous review of available literature that wavers around TQM practices in libraries for quality improvement, it is evident that TQM and allied related names that are used by some libraries, *i.e.*, Quality Assurance, Continuous Quality Improvement, User Satisfaction, etc. are best practices that must be exhibited for effective services to be offered in academic libraries. While it is indisputable that TQM is a concept that is geared toward achieving excellence, success stories may vary in relation to the application of TQM principles across libraries. Hence, employees in academic library settings that are practicing TQM principles may be doing the same job as they were doing previously, but in a different way because improving quality does not mean additional responsibility. Rather, it implies improving the way things are done continuously. However, it has become a reality that service improvement is not only desirable but necessary for the growth and sustainability of effective service delivery, and the application of TQM to academic libraries in the 21st century.

References

Accardi, M. T., Cordova, M., & Leeder, K. (2010). Reviewing the library learning commons: History, models, and perspectives. *College and Undergraduate Libraries.* 17(2/3), 210-329.

Barone, A. (2021). Total quality management (TQM). https://www.investopedia.com/terms/t/total-quality-management-tqm.asp.

Collins English Dictionary (n.d.). Principle definition and meaning. https://www.collinsdictionary.com/dictionary/english/principle.

Dahlgaard, J.J., Kristensen, K., & Kanji, G.K. (1999). Fundamentals of total quality management. Chapman & Hall, London.

Dale, B.G. (1999). Managing quality. Oxford: Blackwell Publishers.

Dixit, P. (2010). Total quality management in libraries: An overview. *International Journal of Librarianship and Administration*, 1(1), 49-53.

Hellsten, U., & Klefsjo, B. (2000). TQM as a management system consisting of values, techniques and tools. *The TQM Magazine*, 12, 238-244.

Julnes, P. L. (2016). Total quality management. In: Farazmand, A. (Eds). *Global encyclopedia of public administration, public policy, and governance*. Springer, Cham. https://doi.org/10.1007/978-3-319-31816— 5_1872-1.

Kiriri, P. N. (2018). Service delivery: The perceptions of users' of library services in a private university in Africa. *European Journal of Multidisciplinary Studies*, 3 (4). 221-231.

Kumbar, R. D. (2004). The importance of marketing and total quality management in Libraries. *Electronic Journal of Academic and Special Libraries,* 5(2-3). http://southernlibrarianship.icaap.org/content/v05n02/kumbar_r01.htm on 13th June, 2021.

LISBDNETWORK (2018). Total Quality Management (TQM). http://www.lisbdnetwork.com/total-quality-management-tqm/.

Maske, D. B., & Khiste, G. P. (2016). Application of total quality management in libraries. One day national conference on advancement and challenges for college libraries in IT era.

Milakovich, M. E. (2006). From quality control to continuous improvement. In Improving service quality in the global economy: Achieving high performance in public and private sectors. Auerbach: Boca Raton.

Moghaddam, G. G., & Moballeghi, M. (2008). Total quality management in library and information sectors.

Munla, M. (2008). The evolution of total quality management (TQM). https://www.grin.com/document/540522.

Nitecki , D. A., & Hernon, P. (2000). Measuring service quality at Yale University's Libraries. *Journal of Academic Librarianship*, 259-273.

Reid, D., & Sanders, N. (2020). Operations management: An integrated approach, 7th Edition. Hoboken: Wiley & Sons.

Saur, K. G. (2007). IFLA library building guidelines: Developments & reflections. K. Latimer & H. Nieegard (Eds.).

Shabarawi, A. (2004). Practical guide to the application of Total Quality Management in an Arab Company. Cairo: Scientific Information.

6

MOOCS in Library and Information Science: A Study of SWAYAM Portal

Sonia Bansal[1] and Suniti Bala[2]

[1]Guru Angad Dev Veterinary and Animal Sciences University, Ludhiana- 141 004
[2]Punjab Agricultural University, Ludhiana-141 004

ABSTRACT

As we all know that emergence of internet has completely changed the way of transferring knowledge. Online videos and lectures have been adopted by the online educational community to meddle into the MOOCs massively to disperse the knowledge. No field has remained untouched from MOOCs. This is basically a study on the available MOOCs in India in Library and Information science.

Keywords: MOOCs, Massive Open Online Course, SWAYAM, Library and Information Science.

1. Introduction

Dave Cormier devised the term Massive Open Online Course (MOOC) in 2008 to describe an open online course "Connectivism and Connective Knowledge" designed by Siemens and Downes. University of Manitoba offered MOOC for the first time in 2008 formally as a credit course to regular students and informally with enrolment open to anybody in the world free of cost. Since then, there is proliferation of MOOCs worldwide. To bridge the digital divide, universities, higher educational institutions and faculties are developing MOOCs to deliver best teaching and learning resources to the learners all over the world. Nowadays, MOOCS have been emerged as a best learning platform for the students who wish to enhance their knowledge and can study at their own in their own setup. In recognition of the escalating popularity of MOOCs, 2012 was declared as the Year of MOOCs by New York Times. Around 16.3K MOOCs were available worldwide by the end of 2020.

MOOCs are the free, open, online courses that allow unlimited participation to geographically dispersed learners. MOOCs usually include discussion on various forums, lecture handouts video lectures and a regular assessment in the form of online questions and assignments. Initially, MOOCs were delivered free, while some providers do charge a fee in exchange for a certificate which isprovided after attending all the lectures and appearing in the periodic assessment of the course.

2. MOOCs in Library and Information Science

School of Information Studies, Syracuse University offered a MOOC on "New Librarianship Master Class" during July and August 2013. In fall 2013, Sant Jone State University's (SJSU) School of Information offered its first comprehensive, open online course, the "Hyperlinked Library" MOOC. This MOOC was designed and delivered as aa prospect for practical development for information professionals and students of Library and Information Science. SJSU offered its second MOOC on 'Emerging Future: Technology Issues and Trends MOOC' dedicated on latest trends in technologyand developing the skills in September2014. Coursera in September 2013 and in July 2014 delivered a course on Metadata which was developed by North Carolina University. A course on "Library Advocacy Unshushed" developed by University of Toronto was offered by edX in 2014 and again in February 2015.

Duke University offered a MOOC on "Copyright for Educators and Librarians" on Coursera platform in 2018. In previous years, edX platform has carried out MOOCs expounded by University of Michigan,focussingon management of Public Libraries which comprise, ascertainingpublicrequirements for this purpose, managing a distinct and full-fledged workplace for public libraries, human resource management, financial management for public libraries, overall infrastructure management, preparing the well-of planning for public libraries, generation of funds, writing for grants for public libraries and marketing the public libraries and generating public relations. A MOOC on "Academic Literacy" was delivered by Coursera in 2018. European Multiple MOOC Aggregator (EMMA) offered a MOOC on "Digital Libraries in Principle and Practice" expounded by Universita Degli Studi di Parma.

3. Completion Rate in MOOCs

The completion rate of MOOCs is very low and this has been confirmed by several studies. Inspite of rapid growth and growing popularity of MOOC courses, massive dropout rate is one of the biggest challenege. Kolowich agreed that "Massive open online courses have gained renown among academics for their impressive enrolment figures and, conversely, their unimpressive completion rates". According to Pursel, "MOOCs typically have low completion rates, at least when compared with traditional courses, as this course delivery model is very different from traditional, fee-based models, such as college courses". The same is the case with MOOCs in Library and Information Science.

In "New Librarianship" MOOC 2405 students enrolled of which only 232 completed the course. It clearly shows that completion rate of the course is 9.65%, whereas the dropout rate is 90.35%. Similarly, a course on metadata received massive response with enrolment of 27623, besides; only 5% students completed this course.

4. MOOCs in India

MOOCs in India were initiated by National Digital Repository and eGyanKosh by IGNOU was the first step. A One Stop Education Portal Sakshat launched by Ministry of Human Resource Development was inaugurated by the then President of India Dr. A.P.J. Abdul Kalam in 2006. This portal was launched to provide an extensive range of knowledge resources, examination alerts, sample papers, educational views, and other useful links on the web to the users of colleges, central and state universities. It includes electronic books, electronic journals, digital repositories and digital librariesto facilitate the students to interact with the faculties in real time via e-mail, discussion forums, blogs, and online chatting. MHRD in 2013 launched e-PG Pathshala under National Mission on Education through ICT (NMEICT). It contains curriculum-based high quality audio and video content in 70 subjects. All these initiatives were primarily focused on delivery of e-content to the students who have been deprived of joining the conventional mode of education.

Followed by Indian Institute of Delhi, Indian Institute of Bombay was the initiator to propose three courses on edX,.Indian Institute of Technology, Kanpur has been offering MOOCs since 2012 using mooKIT management system. Birla Institute of Technology (BITS) Pilani, Rai University, Visvesvaraya Technological University (VTU), Lady Sri Ram College (New Delhi), Bluebells Schools International (New Delhi), Learning Links Foundation are also offering MOOCs in numerous disciplines.

In India, MOOCs are very popular among college students and the students who have recently completed their graduation, and the students who are ready to pay for certificates. Ministry of Human Resource Development (MHRD) took a step forward by launching a MOOC platform named as SWAYAM (Study Webs of Active-learning for Young Aspiring Minds). Initially SWAYAM offered three different courses-one from UC Berkeley's Umesh Vazarani's and two courses from IIT, Bombay. The SWAYAM platform is based on open EDX. It is specially planned to help students from distant and inaccessible areas, college dropouts as well asthe professionals. The University Grants Commission (UGC) permittedthe educational institutions to offer 40% of the total coursesthrough the online credit course via the SWAYAM platform, which are being conducted in a semester for a particular programme. These guidelines further stated that, "No university shall refuse any student for credit mobility of courses earned through SWAYAM platform".

Table 1: List of MOOC Providers

MOOCs Provider	Type	Company/ University/ Person	Headquarters	Year of Foundation
ALISON	Commercial	Mike Feerick	Ireland	2007
Canvas	Commercial	University of Utah	USA	2008
Coursera	Commercial	Stanford University	USA	2012
EduOpen	Non-profit	Govt. of Italy	Italy	2016
edX	Non-profit	MIT, Harvard University	USA	2012
eWant	Non-profit	National Chiao Tung University	Taiwan	2013
FutureLearn	Commercial	The Open University	UK	2012
K-MOOC	Non-profit	Ministry of Education	Korea	2015
OpenHPI		HassoPlattner Institute	Germany	2012
Open2Study	Commercial		Australia	2013
Peer to Peer University	Non-profit	Hewlett Foundation and the Shuttleworth Foundation	USA	2009
POLHN	Non-profit	WHO	Western Pacific Region	2005
SWAYAM	Non-profit	Govt. of India	India	2015
Thai MOOC	Non-profit	Thailand Cyber University	Thailand	2017
Udacity	Commercial	Stanford University	USA	2012
Udemy	Commercial		USA	2010
WizIQ	Commercial	IIT, Delhi	India/USA	2007
XuetangX	Non-profit	Tsinghua University	China	2013
Open Yale Courses	Non-profit	Diana E. E. Kleiner, Yale University	USA	2001

The above table lists famous MOOC providers worldwide. Among these, Coursera, edX, and Future Learn are famous MOOC providers. A report by Class Central also confirmed that Coursera (35.6%) was leading MOOC provider, followed by edX (18.1%).

According to a report published by Class Central, the year 2015 was a turning point in the history of MOOCs as large number of students enrolled in MOOCs than in the previous three years combined (https://nitor.icef.com/2016/01/mooc-enrolment-surpassed-35-million-in-2015/). The pandemic further boosted online education and in 2020, MOOCs crossed 180 million learners, excluding China (https://www.classcentral.com/report/mooc-stats-2020/).

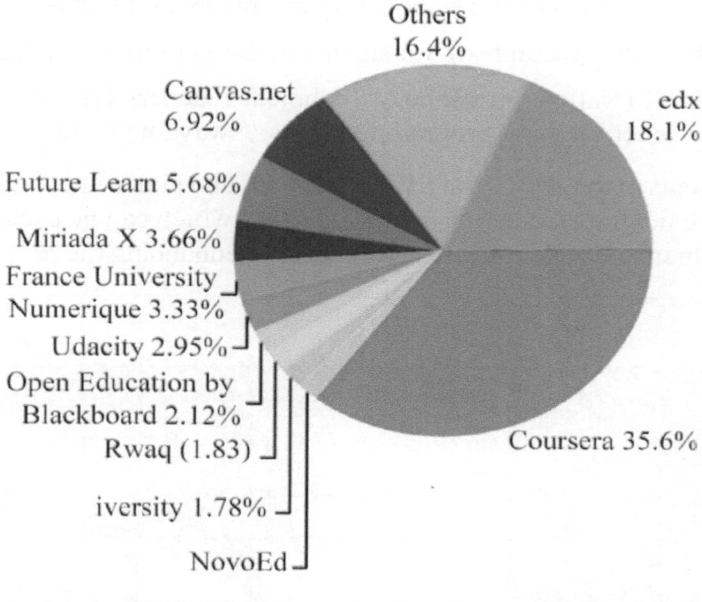

Source: https://monitor.icef.com/2016/01/mooc-enrolment-surpassed-35-million-in-2015/

5. SWAYAM Platform

In order to cope up the technological gap in the nation, Government of India (GOI) launched SWAYAM (Study Webs of Active Learning for Young Aspiring Minds) in 2017 to achieve equity, access and quality in education. The main aim of launching SWAYAM is to provide the best teaching opportunities and guidance to the learners who have hitherto remained untouched by the digital revolution. Nine National Coordinators were assigned to ensure the display and delivery of thestandardized content. Nine Coordinators include.

1. AICTE (All India Council for Technical Education) for self-paced and international courses

2. NPTEL (National Programme on Technology Enhanced Learning) for Engineering
3. UGC (University Grants Commission) for non-technical post-graduation education
4. CEC (Consortium for Educational Communication) for under-graduate education
5. NCERT (National Council of Educational Research and Training) for school education
6. NIOS (National Institute of Open Schooling) for school education
7. IGNOU (Indira Gandhi National Open University) for out-of-school students
8. IIMB (Indian Institute of Management, Bangalore) for management studies
9. NITTTR (National Institute of Technical Teachers Training and Research) for Teacher Training programme (https://swayam.gov.in/about).

The contents of the MOOCsat SWAYAM portalare aimed at pursuing the courses which are not the elementof some syllabi and which can be used as knowledge enhancementand training courses and help in enhancing the professional skills.

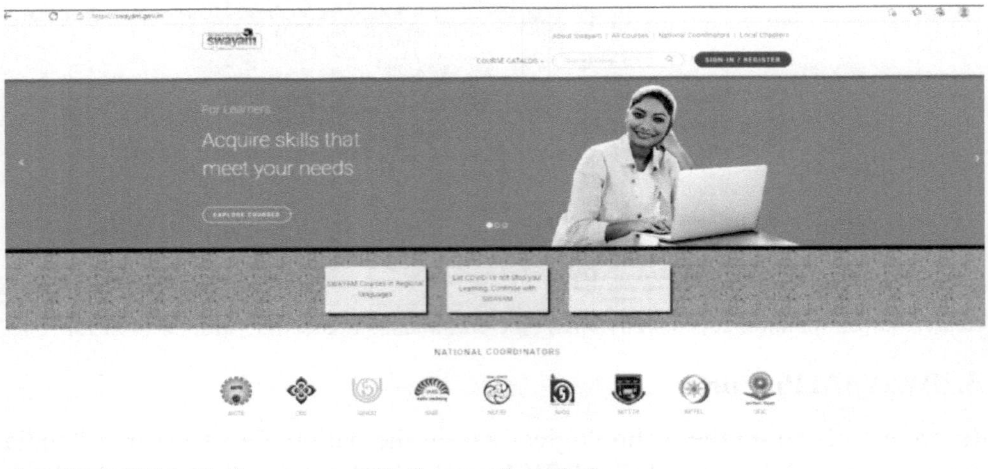

6. MOOCS in Library and Information Science

Library science is the study of librarianship which makes the aspirants to learn the organization and dissemination of knowledge. It is a very challenging profession as information to circulate faster and librarians have to develop their competencies with the changing needs of the users. In this phase, MOOCS may improve the applied knowledge of the professionals as well as the new-comers in this field. Following MOOCS on SWAYAM portal are available in India:

Title	Author	University/ Institute	Duration	Level	Language	Credits	Enrolment	Free/ Paid
BLI-221: Library Information and Society	Dr. Jaideep Sharma	IGNOU	12 weeks	Postgraduate	English	4	25	Free
BLI-222; Information Sources and Services	Dr. Archana Shukla	IGNOU	12 weeks	Postgraduate	English	4	328	Free
BLI-223; Organising and Managing Information	Dr. Jaideep Sharma	IGNOU	12 weeks	Postgraduate	English	4	317	Free
BUI-013: Information Sources and Library Services	Dr. Archna Shukla	IGNOU	12 weeks	Diploma	English	4	2323	Free
Digital Library	Dr. Jagdish Arora	CEC	15 weeks	Postgraduate	English	5	644	Fre
Koha Library Management System	Prof. Kannan Moudgalya	AICTE	12 weeks	Undergraduate / Postgraduate	English	2	2991	Free
Library Automation and Digitisation	Prof. Uma Kanjilal	IGNOU	12 weeks	Diploma	English	4	2880	Free
Sr.Secondary: Library & Information Science	Ms. Manju Chrungu	NIOS	24 weeks	School	English	10	416	Paid

Only a few courses are available in this field, but of course from basic to advance. Advanced courses, *i.e.*, on digital libraries and on Koha open source software) are more popular in the field as being enrolled by maximum number of candidates. Most of the courses on SWAYAM are being hosted by IGNOU and the duration is three to six months. Most of the courses are postgraduate programmes, only one course has been found for school level. Overall, it can be adjudged that this stream is not completely neglected and the qualified community is trying to train others to upgrade this field but still more emphasis is required to produce MOOCS such as on practical aspects of digitization, reference management tools, website designing, *etc.*

7. Summing Up

Although the concept of MOOCS is prevalent since more than one decade, but nowadays when the community is locked at their homes due to pandemic period of COVID-19, the students are able to join the intensive education programmes in the comfortable environment and timings. The equal opportunities are available for all who are keen to learn and study and there is no binding of number of seats. The only need is to introduce more advanced courses in the field to train the library community to learn information organization and dissemination in the modern and a fast-pace changing era.

References

Anders, George (2015). India Loves MOOCs. https://www.technologyreview.com/2015/07/27/166992/india-loves-moocs/

Bast, F. (2015). Science information resources. *Science Reporter*, 52(10), 40-43.

Claire Sewell (2014). The MOOC library degree. http://www.librarianintraining.com/2014/12/the-mooc-library-degree.html

Coursera (n.d.). Academic literacy. https://www.coursera.org/learn/academic-literacy?action=enroll#instructors

Duke University (n.d.). Duke online. https://online.duke.edu/course/copyright-educators-librarians/edX, Courses in professional certificate in public library management. https://www.edx.org/professional-certificate/michiganx-public-library-management

Emerging Future MOOC Participants Discover Innovative Technology and Trends (n.d.). https://ischool.sjsu.edu/about/news/detail/emerging-future-mooc-participants-discover-innovative-technology-and-trends e-PGPathshala (n.d.). https://epgp.inflibnet.ac.in/

Fini, A. (2009). The technological dimension of a Massive Open Online Course: The case of the CCK08 course tools. *International Review of Research in Open and Distance Learning,* 10(5), 1-26.

Guidelines for developing online courses for SWAYAM. https://storage.googleapis.com/swayam1-pub-data/wqimgtest_f8b95943-b963-49b9-85ed-416f2e15d1b4.pdf

https://educationaltechnology.net/massive-open-online-courses-moocs-definitions/

https://ischool.sjsu.edu/post/hyperlinked-library-mooc-0

https://whatis.techtarget.com/definition/massively-open-online-course-MOOC

Jeffrey Pomerantz (2013). Data about the Metadata MOOC, Part 1: Student Activity. https://jeffrey.pomerantz.name/2013/11/data-about-the-metadata-mooc-part-1/

Jeffrey, Pomerantz (2013). Data about the metadata MOOC, Part 4: Completion. https://jeffrey.pomerantz.name/2013/11/data-about-the-metadata-mooc-part-4/

Kizilcec, R.F., Piech, C., & Schneider, E. (2013). Deconstructing disengagement: Analyzing learner subpopulations in massive open online courses. In Proceedings of the Third International Conference on Learning Analytics and Knowledge, 170-179.

Lankes, R.D. (2013). New librarianship master class: MOOC statistics. https://davidlankes.org/rdlankes/Presentations/2013/MOOCStats.pdf

Laura, Pappano (2012). The year of the MOOC. https://www.nytimes.com/2012/11/04/education/edlife/massive-open-online-courses-are-multiplying-at-a-rapid-pace.html

Library Advocacy Unshushed (n.d.). https://www.edx.org/course/library-advocacy-unshushed-2

Massive Open Online Courses (n.d.). https://files.eric.ed.gov/fulltext/EJ1015163.pdf

New Librarianship MOOC (n.d.). https://ischool.syr.edu/registration-open-for-new-librarianship-mooc/

Onah, D. F., Sinclair, J., & Boyatt, R. (2014). Dropout rates of massive open online courses: behavioural patterns. *EDULEARN', 14*, 5825–5834.

Prasanna, Bharti (2014). Indian HRD Ministry launches a MOOC platform. https://edtechreview.in/trends-insights/trends/1598-indian-hrd-ministry-launches-a-mooc-platform-swayam Pujar, Shamprasad M., & Tadasad, Prahalad G. (2016). MOOCs–an opportunity for international collaboration in LIS education. *New Library World*, 117(5/6), 360–373.

Pursel, B.K., Zhang, L, Jablokow, K.W., Choi, G.W., & Velegol, D. (2016). Understanding MOOC students: motivations and behaviours indicative of MOOC completion. *Journal of Computer Assisted Learning*, 32(2), 202-217.

Sakshat (2006). New e-Learning programme launched in India. https://egov. eletsonline.com/2006/10/sakshat-new-e-learning-programme-launched-in-india/

Seaton, D. T., Bergner, Y., Chuang, I., Mitros, P., & Pritchard, D. E. (2014). Who does what in a massive open online course? *Communications of the Acm*, 58–65.

Shah, D. (2020). By the numbers: MOOCs in 2020. https://www.classcentral.com/report/mooc-stats-2020/

Steve, Kolowich (2013). Coursera takes a nuanced view of MOOC dropout rates. https://www.chronicle.com/blogs/wiredcampus/coursera-takes-a-nuanced-view-of-mooc-dropout-rates

The Economic Times, IIT Bombay Launches its First MOOC Courses on the edX Platform. https://economictimes.indiatimes.com/industry/services/education/iit-bombay-launches-its-first-mooc-courses-on-the-edx- platform/articleshow/35063730.cms? from=mdr

University Grants Commission (Credit Framework for Online Learning Courses through Study Webs of Active Learning for Young Aspiring Minds) Regulations, 2021. https://www.ugc.ac.in/pdfnews/2727945_SWAYAM-Regulations-2021.pdf

Yuan, L., & Powell, S. J. (2013). MOOCs and open education: Implications for higher education.https://e-space.mmu.ac.uk/619735/1/MOOCs-and-Open-Education.pdf

7

Open Educational Resources An Insight into Indian Initiatives

Madhu Midha

I.K. Gujral Punjab Technical University, Jalandhar, Kapurthala Highway Kapurthala, Punjab – 144 603

ABSTRACT

There is a tremendous growth in the open educational resources in the recent past and large number of universities and academic organisations are making their resources freely available over the internet which has become a significant source of open educational content. Open education movement are built on the belief that anyone can use, access, reuse and redistribute these educational resources without any constraints. These Open education movements are helping educational community worldwide in making education more accessible and in making it more effective. In this chapter effort has been made to provide an overview of the history and emergence of open educational resources' movement. This chapter also explains the various characteristics and sources of open educational resources. This chapter will help the libraries and librarians to know about open educational resources initiatives and to incorporate them in their libraries for effective resource delivery and disseminations.

Keywords: ICT, OER, Open educational resources, Digital resources, Digital repositories.

1. Open Educational Resources

The Open Educational Resources is a combination of three words Open + Educational + Resources. Which means those electronic resources which are covering educational content *e.g.* Textbooks, lecture notes, course material, full courses etc. and are openly available to teaching and learning community means without any cost freely available to use, adapt and to reuse it.

The term open educational resources are most commonly understood in many different ways by the different communities and users. The open educational resources are usually online educational content like open source and that content is available with open license (mostly available with creative commons license). The most common synonyms used for open educational resources are open content, open learning objects and open learning resources.

Open education resources refer to all those educational materials used for the purpose of formal teaching and learning encompasses all types of course materials, textbooks, research data, Images, videos, open software, games, Audio/ Video lectures, research papers, simulations, and research outputs etc. that are available in digital format and that are free of cost available to all.

There are two main characteristics of OER: 'Libre' and 'Gratis'. Open Educational Resources are learning content that is 'Libre' (openly licensed) and 'Gratis' (free of cost/charge) at the same time.

'Libre' means content that is available with open license (Fully licensed or partially licensed). All content that is available in public domain are also referred under this category.

This availability of OER with open license make the use of OER much easier which otherwise is restricted or refrained due to copyright infringements. This open license grants permissions to users to use the content, remix it, revise it, readapt it, redistribute or share it depending upon the type of license applied to that particular content.

'Gratis' means content that is free of charge digital content but copyrighted, which means users can use this digital content free of cost but if they want to reuse, remix, redistribute or share *etc.* then they need to take the permission from the copyright holder.

Gratis or free of cost may include individual educational content or full course material etc (*i.e.* MOOCS or online courses etc).

William and Flora Hewlett Foundation (2008) has described "OER are teaching, learning, and research resources that reside in the public domain or have been released under an intellectual property license that permits their free use or re-purposing by others. OER include full courses, course materials, modules, textbooks, streaming videos, tests, software, and any other tools, material or techniques used to support access to knowledge".

UNESCO (2002) has explained OERs as "... technology-enabled, open provision of educational resources for consultation, use and adaptation by a community of users for non-commercial purposes. They are typically made freely available over the web or internet. Their principal use is by teachers and educational institutions to support course development, but they can also be used directly by students. Open Educational Resources include learning objects such as lecture material, references and readings, simulations experiments and demonstrations as well as syllabi, curricula and teachers' guide."

2. History and Emergence of Open Educational Resources

Resource sharing among libraries is very common from many decades. In recent past, two milestone initiatives in open education movement OER and MOOCS have significantly influenced and transformed the education system globally.

Many factors played an important role in the emergence and introduction of open educational resources such as availability of large number of resources in digital format, open access resources, open source softwares, government initiatives and projects, universal missions on digital literacy and education for all, price hikes for textbooks and subscribed contents and budgetary constraints for libraries motivated the librarians and libraries in adopting and providing access to open educational resources.

Both the open access movement and open educational resources movement has grown simultaneously. In open access movement some initiatives were the key points such as Budapest open access initiative in 2002, Bethesda open access publishing statement in 2003, Berlin declaration on Open access in 2003, *etc.*

The open educational resources movement has grown at global level consistently due to various international organisations sincere efforts and initiatives, policies, guidelines and declarations. Such consistent initiatives and projects gave a remarkable impetus in stimulating open educational resources movement and played an important role to make it a universally renowned movement. A brief about emergence of open resources movement is mentioned below:

Earlier, the open solutions series was started with GNU project. This project was started by Stallman with a vision to provide free software, he initiated a mass collaboration project under the aegis of GNU project and later he instituted free software foundation.

The term Open-source software was coined by Eric Raymond and Bruce Perens in the year 1997. Wiley and Gurrell (2009) have described that "the concept, which led to the creation of Open Content license, was based on the principles of free/open-source software and the intent of using it in the case of educational materials and other contents".

In the year 1996, California state university initiated the project Merlot. It was the very first website where the teachers can share their learning material freely and that educational material could be used, searched and evaluated by other teaching communities also. Later, the term Open content was introduced by Wiley in the year 1998.

"Universal access to all knowledge" with this mission the Internet Archive was established in the year 1996. The collection consists of millions of books and it fetches billions of downloads per month.

Similarly, like Merlot project, Rice University started their project Connexions (presently named as OpenStax). This Connexions project, an educational content repository was started in 1999.

In 2000, teachers of eight South African countries initiated the project STAMP 2000+ to collaborate and share free resources and teaching materials in Science, Math and technology for free use by other commonwealth teachers.

Then Wikipedia came in the year 2001. Wikipedia is one of the utmost popular website and has a large collection of free articles that includes about 40 million articles and the content is available in 290+ languages.

The other educational institution which played a major role in Open Educational Resources movement is MIT. In 2001, MIT announced Open Courseware (OCW) initiative. This one pioneer initiative inspired many other universities around the world to make their educational content freely available for everyone which resulted in formation of open courseware consortium.

William and flora foundation funded MIT Open course ware project later it has also sponsored many other open educational resources initiatives in different countries.

Inspired by Stallman's Free Software Foundation Larry Lessig founded Creative Commons in 2001. This movement proved as a major milestone in the promotion of open content phenomenon. Like Stallman's GNU GPL (General Public License) project Creative Commons started Open Publication Licenses (OPL). These licenses were developed for the free and easy use of variety of creative works.

In 2002, UNESCO's forum on the impact of Open courseware for higher education in developing countries for the first time used the term "Open Educational Resources".

In 2002 Carnegie Mellon University initiated Open Learning initiative.

In 2005, internet archive in collaboration with yahoo, University of Toronto and University of California established an international network named the open content alliance.

In 2007, Open Society Initiative and Shuttleworth foundation convened a meeting in Cape Town with an aim to stimulate the ideas regarding promotion of open resources, technology aid and teaching practice in education. The outcome came as a published report in 2008 famously known as Cape Town Open Education Declaration. In order to initiate dialogue and to help and improve open education movement's growth, this declaration contains three statements

i) Statement of principle,

ii) Statement of commitment and

iii) The statement of strategy.

In 2010 UNESCO and Commonwealth of Learning jointly initiated the project" Taking the open education resources beyond the OER community: Policy and Capacity"

"Commonwealth of Learning (COL) has been working to promote the development and sharing of quality teaching and learning materials; and, in 2011, it became the first intergovernmental organisation to adopt an open licence policy" (Miao *et al.*, n.d.).

In 2012, in collaboration with UNESCO and with the financial support of the William and Flora Hewlett Foundation, COL played a key role in organising the World OER Congress in Paris. That Congress resulted in the OER Paris Declaration, which explicitly urged governments to release, as OER, teaching, learning and research materials developed with public funds as OER".

In 2018, in honour of tenth anniversary of Cape Town open education declaration the forum created ten key directions to move forward in open education. These ten directions popularly known as CPT+10 in brief is as mentioned below.

i) Communicating Open

ii) Empowering the next generation

iii) Connecting with other open movements

iv) Open education for development

v) Open pedagogy

vi) Thinking outside the institution

vii) Data and analytics

viii) Beyond the textbook

ix) Opening up publicly funded resources

x) Copyright reform for education.

In November 2019, the 40th UNESCO General Conference adopted the UNESCO OER Recommendation which is the only international standard setting framework in this area worldwide.

3. Important Characteristics of Open Educational Resources

i) ***OERs are available free of cost:*** Although there may be some specific objectives to achieve that forced the countries, international organization, societies or educational institutions to initiate the OER projects but the primary and basic objective behind all the initiatives is the free of cost availability of educational resources.

ii) ***OERs are available with pre-approved licenses:*** The second important feature of open educational resources is the availability of the resources with open license which allow users to adapt, reuse and refurbish it. All the resources available in "Open Content" are with some restrictions. The users cannot use, reuse and recreate them due to copyright and intellectual property rights. As OER are available with open license most of the open license are granted by creative commons license that allow teachers to customize them or recreate them according to their local learner's ability, language and culture by giving due acknowledgment to the original author.

iii) ***Another important characteristic of OER is its adaptability:*** In current era, most of the users are equipped with electronic devices like Mobile phones, Tablets, Laptops or desktops etc but the access to high-speed internet is still not very common especially with the remote areas, villages, Hilly areas or areas with special concerns like Jammu and Kashmir etc. In such situations, users can download the open educational resources and use them as and when required later. Downloading facility is available in cases of Open licensed OERs only. The resources other than OERs legally or technically do not allow downloading or reusing of content due to license restrictions.

iv) ***OERS make education affordable to everyone:*** As most of the prestigious educational institutions are putting their educational material free of cost or providing free online course available on their websites. It has made the educational content in reach for everyone. It has benefitted the learning community at large. Those learners who could not join or attend the prestigious institutions like MIT, Harvard, Stanford, Rice, *etc.* due to their geographical, financial, physical or other limitations can now access the educational resources of these institutions freely and can update and sharpen their own educational skills.

v) ***OER Reduces Financial burden:*** Another financial aspect which highly supports the importance of OER from students' perspective is reduced financial burdens. As OER & open textbooks can be easily accessed free of cost and that too in digital format that saves huge amount that students had to spent on purchase of textbooks or on the photocopying charges.

vi) ***OERs as supplementary reading material:*** OERs also acts as a supplementary reading material to teachers and learners both. The teaching and learning community can see, read, use and reuse the educational resources, tools and techniques used and adopted by other prestigious institutions. These help teachers to take advantage and learn from other additional resources apart from their own primary reading materials. Teachers can get new ideas, inspirations and teaching aid from these supplementary educational materials. These additional resources help teachers to get better insight and knowledge on a specific subject. On the other hand, use of OERs as supplementary educational material helps student community in getting better grades and make them more update and knowledgeable than other fellow classmates.

vii) ***OERs provide equal access to quality education:*** Earlier, the access to quality educational content was feasible to only those who get enrolled in educational institutions or to those who have enough funds to busy this educational material. As OER content is free of cost available so it has come in reach of those underprivileged sections of society who earlier could not afford to purchase these materials. OERs help in achieving Universal equality of education & equal access to quality educational material.

viii) ***OERs avoids duplication on the same topic/ Subject area:*** Earlier, teachers were not able to see the teaching materials of other colleagues or teachers. With open course work initiatives, now faculty members from different schools/ departments can see the teaching material of other teachers from different countries/ institutes. This can avoid overlapping or duplication of the same topics they cover. The material produced by teaching community of some prestigious institutions can be used by teachers to cover the same topic. Availability of open educational resources also helps academicians to change their overall teaching pedagogy, encourage them to adopt good educational practices and setting their own global benchmarks.

ix) ***OERs delivers more refined and vast academic knowledge:*** Open educational resources help the students and teachers from low academic level or low ranked institutions to get access to quality content produced by other prestigious institutions teachers. In this way open educational resources provide opportunity to the low ranked institutions learners and teachers to get more authentic, reliable and vast knowledge on the same subject or topic from prestigious teachers. Now, teachers can easily see how the different institutes, teachers and disciplines approaches the same material, such capabilities make it a richer experience for learners and teachers in generating new refined knowledge and many inter and intra departmental collaborations.

x) ***OERs is a great asset to professional education and continuing education programs:*** The main feature of OERs that delivers world class educational material free of cost available to all, facilitate in the development of skills and new knowledge creation that are required for the advancements in society. Open educational resources prove to be a greater asset for advancements in professional education, continuing educational opportunities and for distance or self-learning and help the society in socio and economic mobility.

xi) ***OERs provides universal homogenous quality education:*** Around the globe implausible disparity exists, due to economic and social imbalance which results in uneven resources, academicians and infrastructure availability. Open educational resources provide an opportunity to cater these disparities and universally provide equal homogenous quality education to all.

4. Categories of Open Educational Resources

In the following section a brief has been provided about various categories of open educational resources.

a) Open Courseware

MIT is the pioneer academic university that started the open course ware in 2001. There is a worldwide network of universities and educational institutions that offer open course wares. Open education consortium (www.oeconsortium.org) coursera, and Universia (www.universia.net.en) are two such consortiums.

b) OER websites

Many non-profit organisations or private partners are also involved in helping the society by providing free and open educational resources. There are large number of such open educational resources' websites active both at national and international level. Such as in India Khan Academy and Rai Courseware etc are the private open educational resources platform providing open education in interactive media without any cost.

c) OER Repositories

OER repositories are websites that collaborate and provide many OERs under one platform. These repositories contain open educational resources and their metadata both and managed these metadata through the repository website. The search of relevant open educational resource is made possible through its metadata. On the basis of their location OER repositories have been divided into three categories:

i) ***Local Level OER Repository:*** This type of repository manages the resources and metadata stored in its local repository.

ii) ***External level Repository:*** This type of repository facilitates access through OER websites and provides access to the resources and heterogenous metadata that was stored in various external repositories.

iii) ***Hybrid Repository:*** This type of repository facilitates the access to local repository resources and external repository resources together at one place through its website.

d) OER Collaborations

Many organisations or institutions in collaborations with other organisations work together to meet the common objective of Open educational resources. Many such initiates are supported by UNESCO, William and flora foundation, Creative Commons and European commission etc. in India many such initiates are active with financial or other supports from Ministry oh Human Resource Development or from IITs, IIMs and other universities.

e) OER Government Initiatives

The governments in many countries have agreed upon to put up all that educational material or research outcomes in public domain that have been completed with public money. Apart from this the government in many countries has also initiated many projects and repository to put all the educational content free of cost for the poor and needy students. In India NCERT textbooks is one such noble initiative of government of India.

f) OER Educational Institutions

Many academic institutions at all levels of education whether primary, secondary or higher education are providing Open educational resources. These academic institutions have fostered the open educational resources movement that aims to provide equal access to knowledge for all the students.

Many Institutions are willingly participating in the OER movement as they feel it will improve their academic reputation and will help them in improving their research results and learning materials vide open sharing. Many academic universities and institutions have put up all their educational material like textbooks, course wares, case studied, project reports etc in public domain under Open educational resources for free use by all such as MIT, Stanford University, Rice University, *etc.*

5. Conclusion

Open educational resources are one of the most significant innovations in the higher education systems that facilitate the universal availability and access to scholarly content. In the present era most of the traditional resources are being converted into electronic and ICT enabled resources that includes e-books, e-journals, e-newspapers, e-databases, online database, open source software's and many more such resources. The availability of open educational resources has facilitated the access to scholarly information free to all. Large number of Higher education institutions, universities, academic organisations and intellectuals are contributing and uploading their educational content free of all on different platforms for free and open access by all.

A librarian also plays a major role in providing awareness about these resources to students. The effectiveness of any educational resources depends on the awareness about choosing the right content, skills and methods used to access theses resources, usability of these resources and the learners and educators' attitude towards these resources.

References

Cape Town Open Education Declaration. (2007). *Cape Town Open Education Declaration: Unlocking the promise of open educational resources.* Cape Town: Open Society Institute. Retrieved from http://www.capetowndeclaration.org/read-the-declaration

Miao, F., Mishra, S., & Mcgreal, R. (n.d.). *Open Educational Resources: Policy, Costs and Transformation Perspective on Open and Distance Learning*. http://oasis.col.org

Paris OER declaration (2012).*2012 Paris OER Declaration.* World OER Congress, Paris, June 2012. Retrieved from http://www.unesco.org/new/fileadmin/ MULTIMEDIA/HQ/CI/CI/pdf/Events/Paris%20OER%20Declaration_01.pdf

UNESCO (*2002a*) *open and distance learning: trends, policy and strategy considerations.* Paris: UNESCO. Retrieved from http://unesdoc.unesco.org/images/ 0012/001284/128463e.pdf

UNESCO-COL (2011). *Guidelines for open educational resources (OER) in higher education.*Paris: UNESCO. Retrieved from http://www.col.org/Publication Documents/Guidelines_OER_HE.pdf

Wiley, D., & Gurrell, S. (2009). A decade of development. *Open Learning*, 24 (1), 11–21. Retrieved from http://dx.doi.org/10.1080/02680510802627746

William, & Flora Hewlett Foundation (2016). *Open educational resources initiative.* Retrieved from http://www.hewlett.org/programs/education/open-educational resources.

8

Library Consortia: An Overview

Manju[1] and Bhanu Partap[2]

[1]*Chandigarh College of Architecture, Vidya Path, Sector- 12 D Chandigarh – 160 012*

[2]*Assistant Librarian, Nehru Library, CCS Haryana Agricultural University Hisar – 125 004, Haryana*

ABSTRACT

The advent and implementation of Information and Communication Technology (ICT) in library operations changed the overall information scenario. The format of libraries, information resources and user expectations are completely changing. Similarly, the role of librarian is continuously changing in the digital era. No library can fulfill the informational demands of the users; hence, resource sharing is required between the libraries. Consortiums are developed to enable the institutions to access the rich and scholarly resources at an affordable cost. The present paper discusses the basic concept of resource sharing, consortium types, need, advantages and disadvantages and its role in sharing information.

Keywords: ICT, Consortium, Library consortia, Resource sharing.

1. Introduction

Information and Communication Technology (ICT) has been playing a very important role in every areas of human intervention, and it has changed the way of living life in today's scenario. Similarly, ICT has affected the libraries and it has changed the ways and means of collection building & services in libraries as well. ICT has forced the libraries to change its form from conventional library to electronic library. Due to ICT, types of resources and services, which are currently being provided to the variety of users, have become totally changed. Now, it has being tried to purchase or subscribe the information resources in electronic form by every type of libraries. Electronic resources are those resources, which are available in digital form or in virtual form and to access these resources, it requires computers and or any other electronic platform. Electronic resources can be available in CD–ROMs, Hard Disk or any other external device and in virtual form, and these resources could be accessed through Internet or by ICT means. There are many types of electronic resources, which can be available in any type of libraries. These resources includes e-journals, e-books, e-databases, CD-ROM databases, e-theses, OPAC, e-archives, Internet & Web-based resources, *etc*., which can be made available in any type of libraries.

Information resources available in electronic form are very essential for any big or research libraries in this era of Research and Development (R&D) to meet the research requirements of its users' community. Due to changing scenario and lack of time, library users now want quick and easy access to the information resources. Hence, users prefer to use e-resources as compare to the resources available in physical form. E-resources are easy to use, which can be accessed quickly from anywhere anytime without the time restrictions.

However, due to high cost of e-resources and shrinking budget of libraries day by day, it is not possible for single library or information center to procure all the information resources. Even, single library cannot fulfill all the information needs of users or research fraternity from its holdings. To overcome this issue, library cooperation started a long ago in various form such as Inter-Library Loan (ILL), Document Delivery Service (DDS), and library networks, *etc*. The consortia for the library can be considered as a major step towards the library.

Konnur (2019, p. 105) describes that the "Library Cooperation is one of the oldest practice of our traditional libraries. Sharing the resources from resource rich library to the resource poor libraries is one of the best practices of LIS Profession. As the quantum of information grows and information requirements of researchers and academicians grew in to multifold, the physical transfer of Inter Library Lending could not be sufficient. Further, the format of publishing also grew from print to the digital. Though the fair use clause of Copyright Law allows the libraries to share their resources from one library to other, however, it is not possible to share beyond a limited number of resources. Hence, the mode of cooperation has transformed from print-based environment to digital environment with the introduction of new information technology. The growth of Internet as a new media of information delivery has given rise for proliferation of Web-based full-text online resources. The way of publishing information resources, changing information needs of users, pressure of technological developments and diminishing financial allocations have force the libraries to adopt resource-sharing approach. Due to because of these developments, the libraries are now opting 'shared subscription' or 'consortia-based subscription' to e-books and e-journals worldwide. The library consortia are being formed across the globe with an objective to take advantage of current global network to promote better, faster and more cost-effective ways of providing electronic information resources to the information seekers".

2. What is Consortium?

In common words, a consortium is an association of two or more individuals or organizations having common objectives for cooperation and sharing of information or resources so that each member of consortium can get benefited, and financial resources could be used on cost effective manner.

A consortium can be defined as a strategic alliance of institutes having common interests. The main aim of a consortium is to achieve what members of the group can achieve individually at a relatively low cost (Rangandham *et al.*,2013).

3. Library Consortium

In general, a library consortium is an information inter-change association formed by libraries for co-operatives, networks, alignment, coalition, concomitant or partnership. Consortium can be formed on national, regional & international level.

"Library Consortia is a generic term to indicate any group of libraries that are working together towards a common goal, whether to expand cooperation on traditional library services such as collection development or electronic information services. It is now used perhaps too broadly and encompasses everything from formal legal entitles to information groups that come together solely to achieve better pricing for purchasing electronic information" (Hirshon, 1999).

A library consortium provides a connection of common goals to the libraries to help their users for fulfill their needs. In consortium, a partner library can easily exchange their information resources to other partner libraries, and similarly can use the information resources of other partner libraries to help its users' requirements. In library consortium, member libraries can share different types of resources such as catalogue, OPAC, e-resources and other library services.

4. Need for Library Consortia

It is primary objective of the library to provide up-to-date and nascent information to the users to pursue academic and research activities. Furthermore, it is essential for forming a group of libraries/ institutions, which are having common interest to share their resources.

Some of the reasons for need of library consortia are given as follows.

4.1. Information Explosion

Due to innovations in ICT and extensive R&D activities, information is been generating tremendously worldwide, hence, it is not possible to procure and manage the huge information for a single library. So a consortium is needed to resolve the associated issues.

4.2. Changing Needs of Users

In today's scenario, users' informational requirements have been changing day by day. Now, users want their required information quickly at their place on desktop or palmtop without wasting much time and among, most of them want desired information in online format.

4.3. Limited Budgetary Provision

Provision of budget for libraries is decreasing day by day, which affected the working of libraries badly. A consortium is the only major solution to overcome the problem of financial crunch and to procure maximum information resources.

4.4. Quick Access

Today, in higher educational institutions or scientific research organizations, the researchers hope that they should have access to their required information or resources in electronic form because the contents available in e-form are easy to search and access.

4.5. Time Saving

As all the contents available on consortia are in digital form, hence, it saves precious time of research fraternity during access of contents.

5. Advantages of Consortia

Some of the important advantages of library consortium are as follows.

- Consortium saves time as contents available on it can be accessed 24x7 days from anywhere, anytime
- Optimum utilization of funds by sharing resources through consortium to the partner member libraries
- Consortium can enhanced the spirit of cooperation between the institutions/ organizations for sharing the resources and services in collaboration
- Consortium helps in avoiding duplication of resources and reduces man power in libraries
- It helps in development of common resources database
- Consortium facilitate to build up digital libraries
- Provides access to wider range of electronic resources at lower cost

- Consortium will help in creation of union catalogue
- The consortium acts as a single-window service for a large number of universities with their diverse research and academic interest
- The Consortium, with its collective strength of participating institutions, attracts highly discounted rates of subscription with most favourable terms of agreement for a wider range of e-resources
- Users have immediate access to material previously not subscribed to, at no incremental cost for accessing back files
- It improves the existing library services and reduce the subscription cost
- The research productivity of beneficiary institutions is expected to improve with increased access to international databases and full-text resources
- The Consortium is expected to trigger remarkable increase in sharing of both print and electronic resources amongst participating library
- The Consortium has been opened-up for all other universities/ educational institutions through its "Associate Membership Programme".

6. Disadvantages of Consortia

Consortium has some disadvantages as well, which are as follows.

- Consortia require high initial investments in licensees and information and communication technology
- Internet connectivity is necessary
- Unreliable telecommunication links and insufficient bandwidth
- Absence of a printed copy of Journals
- Lack of standards
- Fear of loss of subscribed contents
- Copyright issues and misuse of research material
- Combination of essential and non-essential journals
- Lack of archiving and back files availability of old journals

7. Types of Library Consortia

There are many consortia are being set up or in existence in India on Regional, National, International level, which are playing very important role in sharing valuable information resources among the member libraries and saves the funds on optimum level. A brief discussion on some of the major consortia is as follows.

7.1. UGC-INFONET

"UGC-INFONET Digital Library Consortium, one of the largest consortium in India, was formally launched in December, 2003 by Honourable Dr. A.P.J Abdul Kalam, the then President of India, soon after providing the Internet connectivity to the universities in 2003 to support education and research. It is an innovative project launched by UGC to facilitate scholarly e-journals to Indian academics through a joint partnership of UGC, INFLIBNET and ERNET. This consortium provides current as well as archival access to 5,790 peer-reviewed journals and 10 bibliographic databases from 23 publishers and aggregators in different disciplines to 160 universities covered under 12B Act of the UGC. Later on, UGC-INFONET Digital Library Consortium has been merged in e-ShodhSindhu Consortium, which is also set up by UGC" (UGC, 2022).

7.2. Indest-AICTE Consortium

The "Indian National Digital Library in Engineering Science and Technology (INDEST) Consortium" was set up in 2003 by the Ministry of Human Resource Development (MHRD) on the recommendations of an Expert Group appointed by the Ministry. The IIT Delhi has been designated as the Consortium Headquarters to coordinate its activities. The Consortium enrols engineering and technological institutions as its members and subscribes to electronic resources for them at discounted rates of subscription and favourable terms and conditions. The Ministry provides funds required for subscription to electronic resources for 62 centrally-funded Government institutions including IITs, IISc Bangalore, NITs, IIITs, IIMs and few other Institutions that are considered as core members of the Consortium. 60 Govt. / Govt.-aided engineering colleges are provided access to selected electronic resources with financial support from the AICTE and 1015 engineering colleges and institutions have joined the Consortium under its self-support category" (Library, IIT-Delhi, 2022). Later on, this Consortium was merged in e-ShodhSindhu Consortium.

7.3. N-LIST

"The project entitled National Library and Information Services Infrastructure for Scholarly Content (N-LIST) was jointly executed by the e-ShodhSindhu Consortium, INFLIBNET Centre and the INDEST-AICTE Consortium, IIT Delhi provides for (i) cross-subscription to e-resources subscribed by the two Consortia, *i.e.*, subscription to INDEST-AICTE resources for universities and e-ShodhSindhu resources for technical institutions; and (ii) access to selected e-resources to colleges. The N-LIST project provides access to e-resources to students, researchers and faculty from colleges and other beneficiary institutions through server(s) installed at the INFLIBNET Centre. The N-List project has four distinct components, *i.e.*, (i) to subscribe and provide access to selected e-ShodhSindhu e-resources to technical institutions (IITs, IISc, IISERs and NITs) and monitor its usage; (ii) to subscribe and provide access to selected INDEST e-resources to selected universities and monitor its usage; (iii) to subscribe and provide access to selected e-resources to 6,000 Govt./ Govt.-aided colleges and monitor its usage; and (iv) to act as a Monitoring Agency for colleges and evaluate, promote, impart training and monitor all activities involved in the process of providing effective and efficient access to e-resources to colleges" (NLIST, INFLIBNET, 2022).

7.4. e-ShodhSindhu

"e-ShodhSindhu Consortium for Higher Education Electronic Resources was formed with merger of three consortia, namely UGC-INFONET Digital Library Consortium, N-LIST and INDEST-AICTE Consortium in December 2015. The main objective of e-ShodhSindhu is to provide current as well as archival access to more than 10,000+ core and peer-reviewed full-text journals (including journals available through N-LIST) and a number of bibliographic, citation, factual and legal databases in different disciplines from a large number of publishers and aggregators to its member institutions including centrally-funded technical institutions, universities and colleges that are covered under 12(B) and 2(f) Sections of the UGC Act" (e-ShodhSindhu, INFLIBNET, 2022).

7.5. NKRC (CSIR Consortia)

The National Knowledge Resource Consortium (NKRC), established in year 2009, is a network of libraries and information centres of 43 Council of Scientific and Industrial Research (CSIR) and 26 Department of Science and Technology (DST) institutes. NKRC was initially formed by National Institute of Science Communication and Information Resources (NISCAIR), New Delhi along with other laboratories of CSIR in the name of "Consortium for CSIR Laboratories for Accessing E-journals", which is now known as NKRC. The consortium started working in June 2002 after an agreement with the Elsevier Science for a period of four years for accessing 1200 journals by all its users. Over a period of time, the Consortium not only grew in terms of the number of resources but also in terms of the number of users as more like-minded institutes evinced interest to join the Consortium. Today, NKRC facilitates access to 5,000+ e-journals of all major publishers, patents, standards, citation and bibliographic databases (NKRC, 2022).

7.6. FORSA

Forum for Resource Sharing in Astronomy and Astrophysics (FORSA) was established in 1981 by Indian astronomy library professionals. "There were seven Founding Members, *viz.* IIAP, PRL, RAC, RRI, TIFR Centre, which came together to formulate strategies for cooperation, collaboration and coordination for resource sharing. Members of FORSA include Indian Institute of Astrophysics, Inter University Centre for Astronomy and Astrophysics, National Center for Radio Astrophysics, Physical Research Laboratory (PRL), Raman Research Institute, *etc*. This is a model where professionals willingly come forward and actively support consortia formation; thereby everyone benefits. It was formed for sharing of resources in areas common to R&D activities. FORSA has realized four consortia, *viz*. Nature Online Consortium; Indian Astrophysics Consortium for physics/astronomy journals of Springer/Kluwer; Consortium for Scientific American online Archive (EBSCO); and Open Consortium for Lecture Notes in Physics (Springer)" (Patil *et al.*, 2007).

7.7. HELINET

"Health Sciences Library and Information Science Network Consortium (HELINET) is the first consortium in the field of health sciences in India, which was conceived by the library of Rajiv Gandhi University of Health Sciences (RGUHS), Bangalore (Karnataka) in 2002. The library of Rajiv Gandhi University of Health Sciences realized that the resources like journals and books are expensive and building a comprehensive collection in every medical college is unaffordable. Thus, the birth of HELINET took place with the motto to network all the libraries under RGUHS for minimizing the cost of acquisition and maintenance of learning resources and maximizing their utilization among the faculty, students and researchers in the colleges and institutions affiliated to the university. HELINET's goal is to deliver information to user's desktop, with round-the-clock-access. About 600+ core international e-journals, 2000+ e-books, 1500+ videos and databases are being subscribed/ procured and provided to students, faculties and research scholar pursuing their studies in various faculties of health sciences of all the respective affiliated colleges under RGUHS" (Manju, 2017).

7.8. DeLCON

"DBT e-Library Consortium (DeLCON) is a unique Electronic Journal Consortium, which is operational since January 2009. The DeLCON was set up by the Department of Biotechnology, Ministry of Science and Technology, Government of India with the objective to promote better, faster and more cost-effective ways of providing information resources to the officials at the consortia member institutions and to strengthen the pooling, sharing and electronically accessing the library resources. The DeLCON have 17 DBT institutions as its members including ICGEB, New Delhi and 18 North Eastern Region (NER) institutions. The Biotechnology Industry Research Assistance Council (BIRAC), New Delhi is also part of DeLCON. Currently, the total members of DeLCON are 35 health science institutions" (DeLCON, 2022).

7.9. ERMED Consortium

National Medical Library's Electronic Resources in Medicine (ERMED) Consortium started in 2008 is an initiative taken by Directorate General of Health Services (DGHS) & Ministry of Health & Family Welfare (MOH&FW), Government of India to develop nationwide electronic information resources in the field of medicine for delivering effective health care. Total 70 state and centrally funded Government Institutions including all AIIMS are selected as its members. There is no membership fee charged from members and the MOH&FW has provided funds required for the purchase of electronic journals under the NML-ERMED Consortium Project. The Consortium is coordinated through it's headquarter set up at the National Medical Library (NML). Total 242 high quality online e-journals are presently purchased from five leading publishers in the field of health and family welfare" (NML, 2022).

7.10. DRDO Consortium

"The DRDO E-Journal Consortium Service came into being with effect from 01 January 2009 covering 448 titles from 7 publishers, namely ACM Digital Library (47 journals, magazines, transactions, *etc*.), ACS (36), AIAA (7), Elsevier Science Direct (195 titles), IEE+IEEE (157 titles plus conferences, standards), Jane's (5), and Science (1). DRDO e-journal consortium facilitates sharing of resources and improving access to information. The resources are shared among DRDO libraries that have common missions, goals, and usage and act on those commonalties. DESIDOC is the nodal agency that administers and monitors the access/subscriptions on behalf of DRDO labs. To evaluate the DRDO e-journals service, a 'Review and Monitoring Committee" under the chairmanship of Chief Controller (R&D) with an overall responsibility for making policies, negotiates with publishers for promoting the consortium has been constituted by DRDO Headquarters. DESIDOC manages the subscription of all electronic resources for all participating laboratories" (Moorthy, 2009 and DRDO, 2022).

7.11. CeRA Consortium (Consortium for e-Resources in Agriculture)

"The Consortium for e-Resources in Agriculture popularly known as CeRA is an e-Consortium of Agricultural Libraries under the Indian Council of Agricultural Research for National Agricultural Research and Education System (NARES) Libraries. The Consortium for e-Resources in Agriculture (CeRA) was established in November 2007 and it is the first of its kind for facilitating 24x7 online accesses of select journals in agricultural and allied sciences to all researchers, teachers and students, policy planners, administrators and extension specialists in NARS through IP authentication. Currently, more than 150 institutions in National Agricultural Research System (NARS) are members of CeRA Consortium consisting ICAR institutes/NRCs/Directorate/Project Directorates/National Bureau, *etc.* and State Agricultural Universities. To put in a nutshell, CeRA acts like a catalyst to enhance agricultural research, education and extension activities of NARS institution in achieving excellence and setting high standards in output and service to the society. To assist researchers to access full text of library-subscribed journals (which does CeRA not subscribe), the Document Delivery Request System has been introduced in CeRA. More than 3000 e-journals to be accessible from CeRA Consortium platform. Apart from this some open access resources, theses, conference proceedings, audio-visuals and e-books are also available on CeRA. After the completion of NAIP project, the Directorate of Knowledge Management in Agriculture (DKMA) of Indian Council of Agriculture Research (ICAR) at Indian Agriculture Research Institute (IARI) is hosting the CeRA Consortium from July 2014 onwards to promote ICT driven technology and information dissemination system for quick, effectual and cost effective delivery of contents to all the stakeholders in agriculture" (CeRA, 2022).

8. Conclusion

The library consortia are helping the students, faculties and the researchers to provide the right information and save their precious time. The consortium has to provide a fruitful service to the users by disseminating their required information with the help of various electronic information resources such as e-journals, e-books and other e-contents. Consortiums based resources are proved very important for the research community. Consortium always tries to bridge the gap between information literate and information illiterate. Furthermore, the provision of consortium has resolved the issue of shrinking budget among the academic institutions. Thus, consortium plays a very important role in imparting educational and research material and fulfils the purpose of the academic and research institutions.

References

DeLCON (2022). http://delcon.gov.in

DRDO (2022). E-Journal Service. https://www.drdo.go.in/e-journal-services

ERMED (2022). ERMED Consortium. http://www.ermed.in

e-ShodhSindhu, INFLIBNET (2022). http://ess.inflibnet.ac.in

HELINET (2022). www.rguhs.ac.in

Hirshon, Arnold (1999). Libraries, consortia and management. *Academic Librarianship*, 25(2), 124-126.

Konnur, P.V. (2019). Library consortia and collaborative resource sharing models for technical university libraries in India. In J.P. Singh Joorel (ed.), *Proceedings of 12th International CALIBER 2019 held from 28-30 November at KIIT Bhubaneswar, Odisha* (pp. 105-113). Gandhinagar- India: INFLIBNET Centre.

Library, IIT Delhi (2022). https://library.iitd.ac.in

Manju (2017). Usage of CeRA consortium among the users Of Chaudhary Charan Singh Haryana Agricultural University, Hisar: A case study. A M.Phil. Dissertation submitted to Department of Library and Information Science, Kurukshetra, Kurukshetra.

Moorthy, A.L. (2009). DRDO E-Journals Consoritum. *DESIDOC Journal of Library & Information Technology*, 29(5), 18-23.

NKRC (2022). http://nkrc.niscair.res.in

N-LIST, UGC (2022). https://nlist.inflibnet.ac.in

Patil, Y.M., Birdie, C., Bawdekar, N., Barve, S., & Anilkumar, N. (2007). Indian consortia models: FORSA libraries' experiences. *Library and Information Services in Astronomy, ASP Conference Series*, Vol. 377, 405-413. http://hdl.handle.net/2248/3922

Rangandham *et al.* (2013). Use of E-Journals through CeRA (consortium for E-Resources in agriculture) by the Students in Acharya N.G. Ranga Agricultural University, S.V. Agricultural College, Regional Library, Tirupati: A study. *International Journal of Contemporary Issues (IJCI)*, 1(2), 35-51.

9

Role of Academic Institution in Promoting Research Integrity: A Peep into the Efforts of Punjab Agricultural University, Ludhiana

Sanjeev Kumar

Mohinder Singh Randhawa Library
Punjab Agricultural University, Ludhiana, Punjab – 141 004

ABSTRACT

Ethical conduct of research is utmost important which form the basis of overall development of society. Academic institutions can play key role in promoting scientific integrity by creating awareness about scientific misconduct and can frame policies to curb scientific misconduct. As a part of course curriculum knowledge about various issues related to academic integrity can be easily passed to young researchers and students of the institution. Awareness programs can play significant role in promoting research integrity for which academic libraries can be the frontrunner. Librarians' role is also changing as they have not limited themselves to traditional services but are also providing web based services to the users. They can support research community by providing services like reference management through the use of reference management tools and data management and preservation services. Faculty development programs are also helping the working librarians to update their knowledge. This article discuss about the concept of academic integrity and role of academic institution in promoting it in general and library in particular. PAU library faculty has taken a lead in raising the awareness of students and researchers about research and publication ethics by teaching this course to as part of the course curriculum to research scholars and post graduate students of the university. It is also facilitating teaching community and researchers in plagiarism checking of the manuscripts through the use of antiplagiarism software.

Keywords: Scientific integrity, Research integrity, Research ethics, User education and research ethics, User awareness programs.

1. Introduction

Scientific research leads to discovery of truth if properly executed and communicated. Honesty and accuracy in research facilitates replication of research by others which forms strong basis for overall development of the society. Ethical practices results in development of sound knowledge in any of the research endeavor. Future research depends upon the present research so it is essential to do it with honesty and integrity. A genuine research work further ensures its replication and benefits to the end user. Research misconduct not only undermines the public trust but also tarnish the image and reputation of research institution.

2. Research Integrity

It means integrity in intellectual work. In other words there should be honesty, fairness and accuracy in conducting the research work.

Office of Research Integrity, U.S has defined Research Integrity as "active adherence to the ethical principles and essential professional standards in conducting responsible research". Responsible research leads to potential impact or benefits to the society or environment.

National Research Council (2002) has defined research integrity as "For individuals research integrity is an aspect of moral character and experience. It involves above all a commitment to intellectual honesty and personal responsibility for ones actions and to a range of practices that characterize responsible research conduct."

Luhman (1979) called research integrity as "System trust" which facilitates researchers, educator, policymakers and public to confidently draw from and build on the research results of others without any need to check for reliability before they use.

3. Academic Institution and Research Integrity

All institutions of higher learning particularly involved in research and development must adopt proper framework for regulating the ongoing research activities. They must have strategic plan for timely assessment of the research programs undertaken by the different departments. Proper leadership, inviting working environment along with proper support and effective mentorship are the key ingredients for promoting academic integrity at institutional level. Leader of the institution should develop a strategic plan within the policy framework of government. Timely enforcement of institutional policies by the leader is effective in maintaining integrity of the research. Congenial working environment free from exploitation and harassment must be ensured by enforcing mandatory institutional policies. Awareness programs should be organized to educate researchers towards research policies of an institution. Further scientists at individual level can contribute by avoiding plagiarism in research proposals. All resources used must be properly acknowledged. Unbiased peer review done by the reviewers of an academic institutions help in publishing quality scientific literature. Scientific development is generally a collaborative activity so cooperation in scientific communication and interaction should be there to share their research findings. Teachers/Scientists as mentor should encourage the researchers/ trainees for further reading literature to enhance their knowledge. They should constantly review the work of researcher(s) and should be constructive in critique of the work. Researchers on the other hand should have dedication towards their research project; ethically conduct all experiments, record keeping, *etc.*

4. Academic Libraries and Research Integrity

Academic libraries being the heart of any institution play significant role in raising awareness about various resources and services. They are better known as information dissemination centers. One of the principle aims of any promotional activity is to enhance the awareness level of user. Information literacy is of prime importance and libraries play major role in making the user information literate through user education programs. Awareness programs can play significant role in promoting research integrity for which academic libraries can be the frontrunner. Therefore the role of libraries in promoting academic integrity can't be overemphasized. Librarians can train faculty members, researchers, and administrators on open access issues due to their sound knowledge in journal evaluation, copyright, licensing issues and searching of resources. Educating the users about open access issues and helping in understanding ethical arguments serve as valuable resource on issues of collaborative research as well as authorship and publication. International organization like Committee on Publication Ethics (COPE) and World Association of Medical Editors (WAME) also emphasize on educating authors, editors and publishers by enumerating their role and responsibilities towards responsible publication. Similarly, libraries of any institution can also play an important role in supporting research by promoting research integrity through their information literacy programs. Special lectures, seminars on emerging issues of research in collaboration with other faculty members of the departments can be organized. As the various organizations at international and national level are working hard to create a culture of ethics, Academic institutions at their level can contribute by formulating policies and procedures to promote the academic integrity.

Proper training of researcher in academic writing and reinforcement of moral rules can play significant role in developing positive attitude towards research and publication ethics. Training courses help in improving the knowledge and understanding about the emerging issues. Educational institutions therefore must have some mechanism which can engage them in activities that can help in raising their awareness about intellectual honesty and ethical conduct of research. Training is considered to be the best available means of preventing misconduct. Offering training as part of teaching course program is common training approach which may vary with regard to content, intensity and delivery mode (Hiney, 2015). In this fast-changing environment information literacy activities of libraries are also changing from bibliographic instructions to supporting research activities of an institution. Ranaweera (2010) also opined that academic integrity, Plagiarism and information source searching and location are essential components of today's user education programs. Libraries are providing reference management and publication ethic services through user awareness and education programs of the library. Librarians are involved in collaborative teaching programs and providing guidance to young researchers and postgraduate students on various ethical issues of research through teaching and extension activities. Training should focus on fundamental norms and if internalized at an early stage would prove useful as it can provide researcher with solid ethical framework within which to work. The main aim is to create the culture of ethics so that it should become way of life. Research misconduct can be reduced through open access publishing as it creates more transparent and open system that allow the researchers to share their findings to much larger audiences.

5. Punjab Agricultural University and Research Integrity

User education program dates back to as early as 1970 in the higher agricultural education institutions. Most of the agricultural universities offer information literacy program as part of their curriculum to graduate and PhD students (Singh, 2014). Libraries are now providing research support services like references management through the use of different reference management tools and data support services to their users. Library faculty is actively involved in taking course on ethical research. Punjab Agricultural University, Ludhiana has taken various initiatives in promoting academic honesty and research integrity. PAU library is the lead centre in this regard.

5.1. Information Literacy Programs

Punjab Agricultural University regularly conducts user awareness and orientation programs to acquaint the new users with the resources and services of the library. Extension lectures about awareness and use of various online resources like CeRA, KRISHIKOSH and other research databases are also organized by the library for the faculty covering different departments of the university. University also offers mandatory research support programs namely PGS-501 and RPE-501 as part of its curriculum to researchers and postgraduate students of the university. These courses are offered every semester to the researchers and postgraduate students of the university. Library faculty is providing guidance and training to the students and researchers of the university about reference management techniques as well as publication ethics through these courses. These courses are helping the researchers in raising their awareness about research misconduct and ways to prevent it. Institutional policies have also been framed with regard to plagiarism.

5.2. Use of Anti-plagiarism Software

Plagiarism is one of the most common forms of research misconduct as it undermines the contribution of an original author. With the advancement of technology easy cut and paste method has resulted in quantity rather than quality publications. Young researchers follow shortcut methods owing to various reasons. Various online Plagiarism detection software (PDS) tools have been developed to detect similarity in the text. Punjab Agriculture University has also implemented TURNITIN software to enhance the quality of research publications. PAU library was instrumental in procuring the anti-plagiarism software for the university. One of the library faculty members was selected as administrator for successful implementation of the software. Training programs were organized for the faculty regarding awareness and use of the software. All thesis submitted to the university and research papers are checked for similarity through this software.

5.3. User Awareness Activities

Various seminars and conferences are organized time to time at university and departmental level to create awareness about ethical practices of research. Specialized lectures on predatory publications were organized for the faculty and researchers by library to create awareness about it.

5.4. Online Webinars

Various online webinars about software tools which can help in research writing, Reference management and plagiarism detection tools were also organized by the library during pandemic period.

6. Conclusion

Honest research and accurate reporting of results build sound foundation for scientific growth and development. It is therefore very necessary to imbibe ethics of science and research in the minds of author, researchers and students involved in research and development. Efforts should be made by higher educational institutions to create culture of ethics so that it may become way of life. Academic libraries being the centre of information and dissemination can play vital role in raising the awareness of user. Librarian's role is fast changing as they are collaborating with teachers in guiding researchers and students to sensitive issue of plagiarism and publication ethics. They are now actively educating the users about open access issues and helping them in understanding ethical arguments through teaching programs of the university which can serve as valuable resource on issues of collaborative research as well as authorship and publication. With their expert knowledge in journal evaluation, copyright and licensing and open access resources they can be better partner with teachers in promoting research integrity and academic honesty among the researchers and students of the university. With this new role image of the library as well of the institution can be improved.

References

Hiney, M. (2015). Research integrity: what it means, why it is important and how we might protect it. *Strasbourg: Science Europe*.

Luhmann, N. (1979), Trust and Power; Wiley: Chichester, UK.

National Research Council (US) & Institute of Medicine (US) Committee on Assessing Integrity in Research Environments. Integrity in Research. In Integrity in scientific research: creating an environment that promotes responsible conduct. Washington (DC): National Academies Press. Retrieved on Jan, 21, 2022 https://www.nap.edu/read/10430/chapter/1

Office of Research Integrity. (n.d.). Definition of research misconduct. Retrieved on Jan, 21, 2022. https://ori.hhs.gov/education/products/ucla/chapter1/page02.htm

Ranaweera, P. (2010). Information literacy programmes conducted by the universities in Sri Lanka. *Journal of the University Librarians Association of Sri Lanka*, 14(1). https://doi.org/10.4038/jula.v14i1.2688

Singh, N. (2014). Attaining Information Literacy: An assessment of Indian Agricultural Universities approach to enhancing Student's Information and Research skills. Available at http://library.ifla.org/1009/1/140-singh-en.pdf.

10

Acquisition Pattern of Libraries

Yogita Talwar

Lovely Professional University Jalandhar, Grand Trunk Road Phagwara, Punjab – 144 001

ABSTRACT

It is very important for every library to have all the resources/materials necessary to fulfil its target. The working of a library can be classified into two forms: dealing with the users and behind the scene. There are numerous different sections in a library divided on the basis of their functions. Most important of these is the Acquisition section. A library's success lies in a well organized acquisition section. Main aim of the library is the contentment of the users. However, collection development is the primary task of the acquisition section which further contributes to user satisfaction itself. It performs the process of selection, procurement and accessioning of reading materials as well as maintains records. It organizes the monetary as well as human resources in such a manner that collection is facilitated more and that too in an economic and less time consuming way. All this is the responsibility of the librarian. Before acquiring the reading materials, the librarian is supposed to decide that which items are actually required in the library and which are to be rejected. A librarian must study the requirements of the library and acquire materials as per the priorities of the institution to achieve its goal.

Keywords: Acquisition, Policy, Role of vendors, Relation between different departments, Bill processing and Selection procedure.

1. Introduction

Acquisition can be regarded as the process of acquiring selected material for libraries and information centers in the form of e-resources as well as print resources. It not only includes acquiring material but also maintaining record of acquisition section. Materials should be selected as per the library's collection development policy. It also includes checking for the bibliographic record before placing the order so as to ensure that no duplication of material takes place. Then selected material is acquired by ordering them for purchase, exchange or gift. Then the material is received, proper quality check tests are done manually, bills are processed, payments is made to vendors, and necessary records related to acquisition are maintained.

First function of the Librarian Technical Services is acquisition followed by cataloging and collection management. Acquisition is also referred as functional department which is responsible for all sort of functions related to obtaining of materials. Small libraries still follow the old traditional system where chief librarian was responsible for taking decisions related to acquisition; however actual ordering was done by the clerical staff. Large libraries of modern era with big collections have enough budgets for maintaining a separate unit for this purpose known as Acquisition Department.

2. Acquisition

Acquisition is the primary and principle management process in a library. The word acquisition actually means qualitative procurement of reading materials after the selection process.

According to Gorman, 1998, "Acquisition concerned with the ordering, claiming and receipt of materials for the library".

2.1. Acquisition in a Small Library

In a school or a college library acquisition unit collects mainly materials related to the curriculum of courses taught at the school/college.

2.2. Acquisition in a Special Library

Special libraries serve as information centers for special type o users. In these libraries such as libraries of business schools, engineering institutions, court libraries etc. consist of the materials that are related to their specific area only such as reports, old and new records, policies, rules and regulation, *etc*. It has been regarded as best bulk communication media.

2.3. Acquisition in An Academic Library

In large academic libraries acquisitions units are mostly organized by the material types to be ordered, generally consisting of rare books section, textbook section, reference section, periodicals section, and further subdivided by the country or region of the world where the materials being requested actually belongs to and can be obtained if the library collects in a number of languages. These libraries provide additional services for higher grade of learning, research and dissemination of knowledge publication.

2.4. Acquisition in a Public Library

Public libraries purchase materials of general interest. These might include materials ranging from that for children to that for senior citizens. These libraries often house materials related to the culture and customs of the very place where it is situated. These can be regarded as social institutions providing services based on books and information for different public groups such as social, political, economic, cultural, *etc*.

2.5. Acquisition in a National Library

National libraries are those which function as 'deposit' libraries either by law or some other means of arrangement. All the considerable publications published in the nation are compulsorily acquired and conserved at a national library. It is funded by the national government. Its function may include comprehensive collection of publications of the nation, compilation and maintenance of national bibliography, etc. It also acts as a copyright depository library. It also disseminates the information through indexing and abstracting services. If any institution or agency does not compile and publish indexes to present research journals, then national libraries take this responsibility. It also prepare and produce abstracts on literature of national interest.

3. Role of Vendors in Acquisitions

In very small libraries like school/college libraries, a single individual orders materials from the vendors however in very large libraries such as university library or public library, a number of vendors are asked for quotations and the materials are ordered from the best option available. While choosing the vendor to purchase materials from, the quality of services like shipping, etc. are also noted along with the price, quality and edition of reading materials. In case the subject specialist is not content with the quality of the material, it can be returned by the librarian.

The functioning of the library is classified in two different forms- public dealing and work behind the scene. Commonly, users don't have much knowledge about the significance of Acquisition services in a library. The main reason behind is lack of opportunity to observe the working of the acquisition section. However, the performance of the library mainly depends on the efficiency of the acquisition department.

4. Objective of the Acquisition Section

The acquisition is the foremost task to be accomplished in a library. It has such a great significance that the most used reading material should be acquired regularly from time to time that too at the least cost possible. Only a library with properly organized acquisition section, experienced staff as well as latest technology can accomplish this task. Some important objectives need to be decided at first for the accomplishment of this purpose. These objectives are different for different types of libraries. Some common objectives are mentioned below:

1. The most basic function of the library is to provide all sorts of reading materials to its users. Therefore it is the responsibility of the library to provide these materials for the satisfaction of the user. Because user satisfaction is one of the major objectives of the library. For *e.g.*, a university library should have adequate collection of research materials for research scholars along with the books related to the curriculum.
2. A library should not only contain learning or study materials, but also have an excess of all other books for the relaxation of the user such as novels, motivational books, *etc*. Books on borderline subjects should also be available in a library so that adequate amount of material is available for research purpose.
3. All reading materials related to the history or traditions of the country or region should also be available. Materials related to the history of the institution could also add a sense of interest in the users. Therefore libraries can be regarded as a repository of rich cultural heritage for the awareness amongst the new generation.

5. Functions of An Acquisition Section

Acquisition is one of the major functions assigned to a librarian in the library. Some of the acquisition tasks performed by an acquisition librarian are listed below:

1. Development of certain procedures to fulfill the requirements of the library.
2. To correspond with the vendors and order required reading materials for the library either in the printed form or in the form of e-resources.
3. To recommend the best books to the faculty for teaching purpose so that the finest quality of education can be imparted.
4. Discussion with the heads of other departments and divisions before placing book orders.
5. To stay informed and look for auctions, rare books and used book dealer's catalogs for getting books at desirable costs.
6. To digitalize the print material or reproduce it when their printing has stopped or their original copies aren't available.

7. To stay in touch with the representatives of different publishers, distributors, collectors, *etc.* who can provide help in enhancement in the collection of the university.
8. To examine print as well as e-resources and recommend their acquisition if required.
9. Supervision of all sorts of gifts and exchanges received by the library.

6. Supplementary Functions of Acquisition Department

1. Preparing Demand Indent files.
2. Preparing files related to orders placed. It is also known as purchase order file (P.O. file). Desiderata list and "In process" files are important for acquisition task.
3. Maintaining receipts of incoming shipments, and, managing and examining them.
4. Packing and returning received materials in case of any discrepancy.
5. Processing of bills after accessioning of books in accession register.
6. Preparing list of accessioned books.
7. Providing information to the recommenders from specific departments about the status of their recommendations.
8. Preparing bills' files for future reference.
9. Place orders and keeping checking on periodicals, *etc.*
10. Contacting and taking feedback from vendors regarding pending orders.

7. Relations with Other Sections

- **Relation with the processing section:** Acquisition section has a very close connection with the processing section as both these sections are interdependent. Acquisition section may take help of processing section in processing books faster so that catalogue always stays up-to-date and it can also prevent processing of same set of books more than once. For avoiding needless duplication, the incharge of the processing section has to keep the incharge of acquisition section updated in case there is any change in classification and cataloguing policies.
- **Relation with the Reference Section:** This section is visited by the users very often in order to consult with the incharge of reference section regarding the issues they are facing. Most of the times, users complain about the lack of materials related to a specific subject. In this case, ordering of materials related to that specific subject can be recommended to the incharge of the

acquisition section by the incharge of reference section. This is an important aspect as the reference section is in direct contact with the users.

- **Relation with the Binding Section:** In order to avoid wear and tear of books, the books in unbounded form are sent to the binding section for binding them. Books with some minor defects can also be sent to binding section for maintenance before forwarding to technical section.
- **Relation with the Circulation Section:** The circulation section and the acquisition section need to maintain a very close relation as circulation section is responsible for informing the acquisition section regarding materials related to which specific title are in demand and how many copies of that title are required.

  The staff of library needs to maintain close relation with the following sections to ensure the smooth working in the library.
- **Selection of books:** Process of selection of books is different for different libraries. Before selecting the books for placing order, a library first needs to check for its budget and the users' common interests, as these factors vary from library to library. Therefore, this is a very accountable job.
- **Tools for selection of books:** These tools include all those resources that need to be acquired on regular basis such as Book trade lists, cumulative book indexes, etc. It is better if a standing order is placed for their acquisition. The library committee should be made aware about all the significant and recent bibliographical tools.

8. Selection Procedure

The librarian orders books keeping in mind the suggestions made by the following:

1. Suggestions of all the Department Heads in the institution.
2. Suggestions of the Library Committee (In case of Public Libraries).
3. Suggestions of library professionals of the library.
4. Suggestions of the users.

Proper consolidated lists and book selection cards are prepared keeping in mind all the above mentioned suggestions collected under numerous subject headings.

- **Receipt of books:** The books are received directly by the library along with the bills in case of a local bookseller. However, if the bookseller/vendor/distributor is not a local one, then the bill of the books is sent along with the railway receipt under the register cover. These bills may be received directly by incharge of the acquisition section or via librarian.

- **Checking of Bills:** The bills are first tallied with the physical material and later with the purchase order that is lying pending in the order processing file. Also a note is prepared specially for noting down the discrepancies, if any. After checking that all the ordered books have been received, its edition and authors are checked and imprints are verified.
- **Collation and Tallying Work:** This includes checking and confirming the prices of the books. Most often, the price of the books is printed on the inner flap of dust cover on title page or on its back. The prices are also compared with the prices on online authentic sites. The prices can also be checked on the publishers'/distributors' catalogues.
- **Accessioning Work:** After the checking and tallying of books physically as well as with the purchase order is over, these are handed over to the person whosoever is responsible for accessioning of books. Accession register is the primary document of every library. In this register, every book is marked with a unique number in a consecutive manner. This unique serial number is known as the Accession number. There are two different accession registers- one for new purchases and the other one for gifted books.
- **Bill Processing:** The process of bill processing is stated below:
  1. Every item received by the library is checked carefully.
  2. It is ensured that every book has been entered in the Accession register and given the unique accession number.
  3. Vendors have charged the approved rates.
  4. It is checked that there is no mistake in calculations.
  5. The bill has been debited to the appropriate budget heads.

9. Conclusion

Collection building is of great importance for a library. A good collection does not build up on its own but needs to be built by great planning and its execution in a systematic manner. This is the main responsibility of the librarian. Proper professional training and experience is required to expertise this task. The foremost thing to keep in mind is designing a suitable policy that can't be copied from any other library as each library has to build up its own different policy depending on their budget, manpower, etc. The process of acquisition includes all the tasks and functions from the screening in the starting to the final selection of materials. It is important to maintain the record of all types of materials that are collected in the library along with their need and the means of acquirement. Heads of other departments may give suggestions to the librarian regarding purchase; however, the final decision is in the hands of the appointed librarian.

References

Librarianship Studies and Information Technology "Acquisition (Libraries)". https://www.librarianshipstudies.com/2015/05/acquisitions.html.

Mittal, R.L (1984). *Library Administration, Theory and Practice*. Delhi: Metropolitan Book Co. https://archive.org/stream/in.ernet.dli.2015.107539/2015.107539.Library-Administration-Theory-And-Practice_djvu.txt

11

ICT-Based Services to the Readers and Access to E-Resources: A Study

Vijay Kumar Bharati

Dr. Bhagwandas Central Library, Mahatma Gandhi Kashi Vidyapith Varanasi – 221002, Uttar Pradesh

ABSTRACT

This study addresses the many ICT-based services provided to readers as well as access to E-resources by Mahatma Gandhi Kashi Vidyapith, University users. It raises awareness of technology in libraries and why it is important to comprehend the usage of ICT in libraries in order to provide better library services and information to users. Essentially, the article describes several technologies and their applications in library operations. The study has discussed how library services are spurred by the use of technology such as OPAC, E-ShodhSindhu, E- books and E-journals, and so on. The current study examines several library activities that make use of ICTs. The goal of this paper is to demonstrate the use of various ICTs and E-resources by user of the university for rapid and easy information retrieval.

Keywords: ICT, Resources and Services, E-Resources, Access, Library Operations.

1. Introduction

With the increasing influence of information communication technology, there has been a rapid change in libraries and their services. Due to Covid-19 also it has become mandatory for libraries to provide their services through ICT. After the invention of ICT and the internet, the collection and services of any library have undergone rapid changes. Today's society has come to be known as the society of knowledge; any library is the superstructure of this society. The university library is the core knowledge center of the university which acts like a heart. The best collection in the central library and its services involves optimum use of physical and online service visibility. The two major regulatory bodies in university education, the UGC and the NAAC are seriously concerned about how to better develop standards for academic libraries. Libraries that have smart readers, e-resources, smart locations, Wi-Fi facilities with a green eco-environment, and smart services can be classified as ICT based libraries. The author explained here to the readers about the study of ICT-based services and access to E-resources for university students. The library has print documents as well as E-resources for access to the students of Mahatma Gandhi Kashi Vidyapith, Varanasi.

2. ICT-Based Services and E-Resources of Central Library

Mahatma Gandhi Kashi Vidyapith Varanasi is a state university in Uttar Pradesh. It was founded on 10 February 1921 by Mahatma Gandhi, Babu Shiv Prasad Gupta, and Bhagwandas during the non-cooperation movement of the freedom struggle. In1995 the name of the institution was changed to Mahatma Gandhi Kashi Vidyapith Varanasi. The university covers its main campus as well as two more campuses and about four hundred colleges affiliated to six districts. It is an important state university of Purvanchal Uttar Pradesh, in which hundreds of thousands of students from both rural and urban places pursue higher education. It offers a variety of professional and academic courses in the arts, sciences, business, law, computing, and management. MG Kashi Vidyapith is currently prospering under the able leadership of Vice-Chancellor Professor Anand K. Tyagi.

The Dr. Bhagwandas Central Library was also established in 1921 along with the establishment of the university. It was earlier known as Bhagwandas Swadhyayapeeth. Dr. Bhagwandas was a renowned philosopher and the first Vice-Chancellor of the university. This library is dedicated to Pandit Jawaharlal Nehru, Jamunalal Bajaj, Acharya J.B. Kripalani was closely associated with many stalwarts of the national movement including Purushottamdas Tandon, Rafi Ahmed Kidwai, Sampoornanand, Lal Bahadur Shastri, and Pandit Kamalapati Tripathi. The mission of the central library is to assist in the creation of new knowledge by acquiring, organizing, and disseminating knowledge resources and providing value-added services. The central library houses a large number of ICT-based services and e-resources such as E-books, J-get Plus Journal, i-Scholar, India Business Insight, Bibliotex India, and E-Shodhsindhu, *etc.* as well as e-contents developed by academician of Mahatma Gandhi Kashi Vidyapith University offers to its students.

3. Objectives

The purpose of this study was to investigate the utilization and understanding of ICT-based services and E-resources of Central Library at Mahatma Gandhi Kashi Vidyapith, Varanasi. The primary objectives were as follows:

- To measure the level of understanding and frequency of usage of various forms of ICT-based services, E-contents and E-resources of central library
- Determine the goals of employing E-resources.
- To identify issues encountered when accessing E-resources.
- Determine the efficacy of E-resources.
- Determine if ICT-based services and E-resources can replace offline services and print resources.

4. Methodology

To achieve the objectives, a systematic questionnaire encompassing all components of the study was created and sent to the concerned students of the central library, Mahatma Gandhi Kashi Vidyapith, and Varanasi. In all, 500 Google forms were sent, with 450 completed questionnaires returned by respondents. The acquired data was evaluated, categorized, and tabulated, and conclusions were drawn as a result of the results.

5. Data Analysis, Interpretation and Findings

5.1 Frequency Distribution of Respondent's Type

The graph 5.1 shows the frequency distribution of respondent's type. It is clear from above graph that 600 questionnaires were distributed to the students and 510 were duly filled and received back. Out of 510 respondents, 250, 170, and 90 questionnaires were received from UG, PG, and Research Scholars respectively.

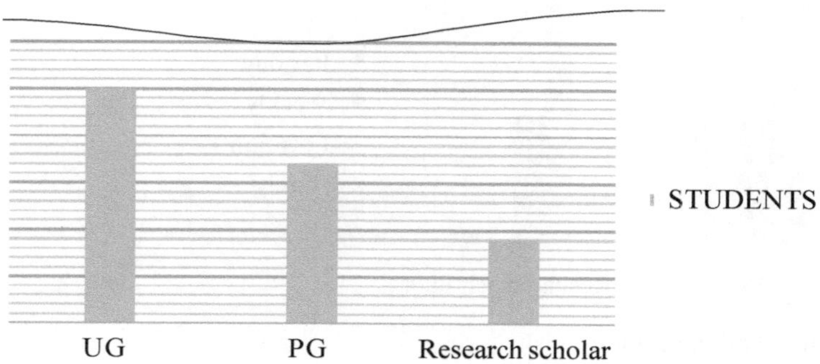

Graph 5.1. Frequency distribution of respondent's type

5.2 Frequency Distribution of Respondent's Gender

The graph 5.2 shows the frequency distribution of respondent's gender. It is clear from above graph that 600 questionnaires were distributed to the students and 510 were duly filled and received back. Out of 510 respondents responded against the questionnaire, of which 130 (25%) were female student and 380 (75 %) were male student.

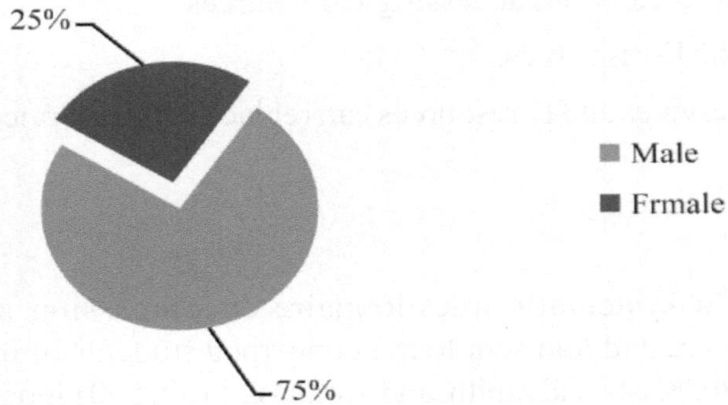

Graph 5.2. Frequency distribution of respondent's gender

5.3 Frequency Distribution of Library Visit

It is observed from the analysis that 25 % of the UG students visit the library daily while 35% visit weekly followed by 30% fortnightly and 10% rarely. Further it is also observed that 40 % of the PG students visit the library daily while 30% visit weekly followed by 25% fortnightly and 5% rarely. At the research level, it is found that 60 % of the research students visit the library daily while 30% visit weekly followed by 05% fortnightly and 05% rarely.

Graph 5.3. Frequency distribution of library visit

5.4 Methods of Searching Catalogue

The graph 5.4 shows the methods of searching catalogue among students of Kashi Vidyapith. It is observed from the analysis that 75 % of the UG students search their books detail from OPAC and 25 % search books details by print catalogue while 80 % of the PG students search their books detail from OPAC and 20 % search books details by print catalogue. At research level, it is also observed that 85 % of the research students search their books detail from OPAC and 15 % search books details by print catalogue.

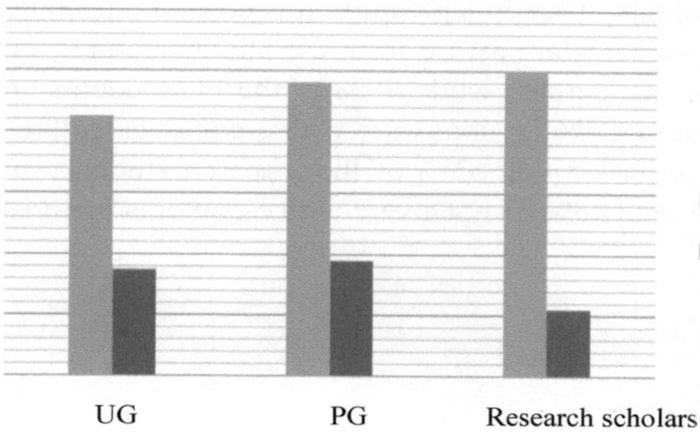

Graph 5.4. Methods of searching catalogue

5.5 Awareness of E-Resources

The graph 5.5 displays the awareness of e- resources among students of Kashi Vidyapith. It is observed from the analysis that 65% of the UG students are aware from e- resources and 35% do not aware with e-resources while 80% of the PG students are aware from e- resources and 20% do not aware with e-resources. At research level, it is also observed that 95% of the research students are aware from e- resources and 5% do not aware with e-resources.

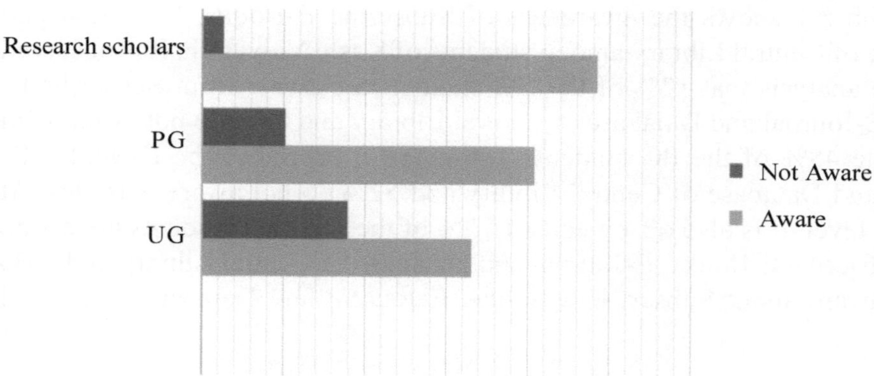

Graph 5.5. Awareness of e- resources

5.6 Awareness with E-Content/Lectures Prepared by University Teachers

The graph 5.6 shows the awareness of e-contents/lectures prepared by our university teachers among students of Kashi Vidyapith. It is observed from the analysis that 92% of the UG students are aware from e-contents/lectures and 8% do not aware with e-contents/lectures while 98% of the PG students are aware from e-contents/lectures and 2% do not aware with e-contents/lectures. At research level, it is also observed that 55% of the research students are aware from e-contents/lectures and 45% do not aware with e-contents/lectures.

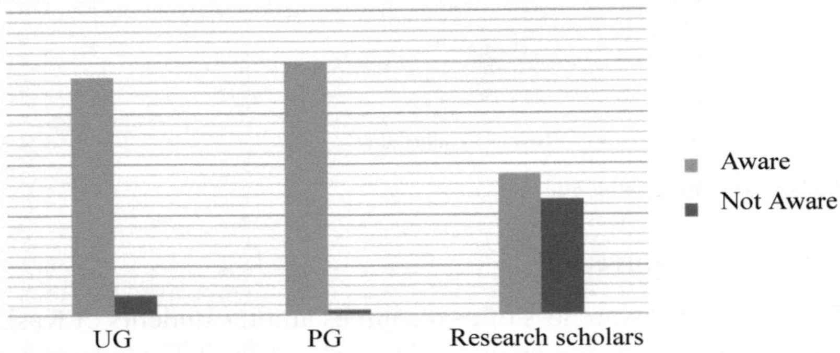

Graph 5.6. Awareness of E-Content/lectures prepared by university teachers

5.7 Awareness with Subscribe E-Books, E-Journal and Database of Central Library

The graph 5.7 shows the awareness of Subscribe E-Books, E-Journal and Database of Central Library among students of Kashi Vidyapith. It is observed from the analysis that 12% of the UG students are aware from Subscribe E-Books, E-Journal and Database of Central Library and 88% do not aware with this while 48% of the PG students are aware from Subscribe E-Books, E-Journal and Database of Central Library and 52% do not aware with this. At research level, it is also observed that 75% of the research students are aware from Subscribe E-Books, E-Journal and Database of Central Library and 25% do not aware about Subscribe E-Books, E-Journal and Database of Central Library.

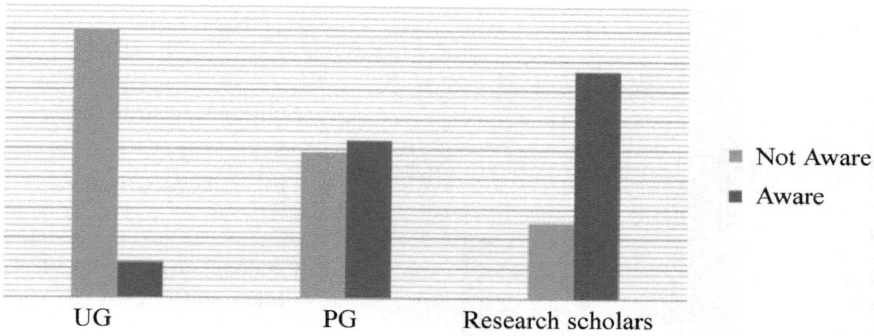

Graph 5.7. Awareness with subscribe e-books, e-journal and database of central library

5.8 Access of Subscribed and Unsubscribed Resources

The graph 5.8 displays the awareness of subscribed and unsubscribed resources among students of Kashi Vidyapith. It is observed from the analysis that 05% of the UG students access of subscribed and 95% access unsubscribed resources while 48% of the PG students access of subscribed and 52% access unsubscribed resources. At research level, it is also observed that 80% of the research students are access of subscribed and 20% access of unsubscribed resources.

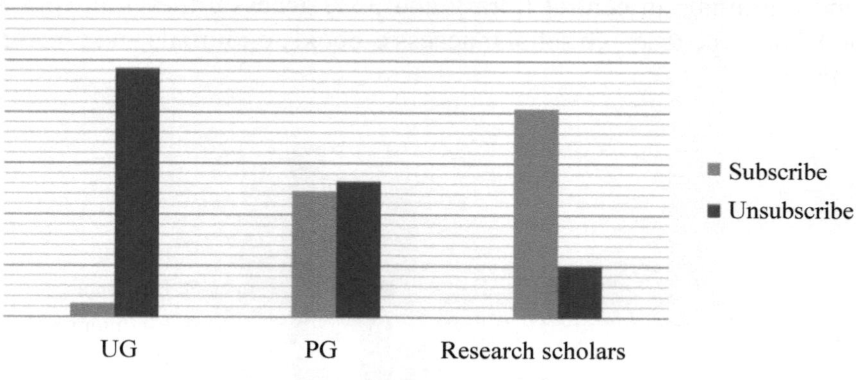

Graph 5.8. Awareness of subscribed and unsubscribed resources

5.9 Methods of Learning ICT Based Services

The graph 5.9 displays the awareness of methods of learning ICT based services among students of Kashi Vidyapith. It is observed from the analysis that 25% of the UG students learn by self and 45% by friends and 20% by library staff while 35% of the UG students learn by self and 35% by friends and 30% by library staff. At research level, it is also observed that 50% of the research students learn by self and 20% by friends and 30% by library staff.

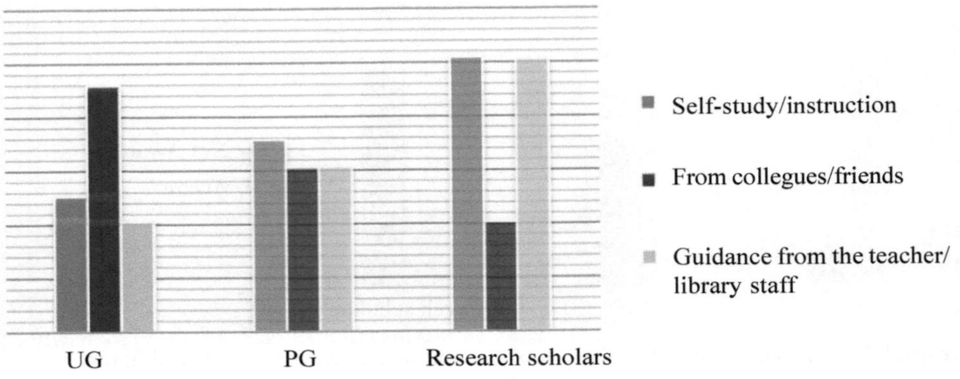

Graph 5.9. Methods of learning ICT based services

5.10 Type of E-Resources Access in Central Library

The graph 5.10 presents the type of e-resources access in central library among students of Kashi Vidyapith. It is observed from the analysis that overall 5% of the UG students access E-resources as e-books, e-journals, etc. in central library while 35 % of the PG students access e-Books and e journals in central library. At research level, it is also observed that 45% of the research students access e-books and e-journals in central library and 35% access e-theses in central library and 80% of the research scholar access e-books, e-journals and e-theses in central library.

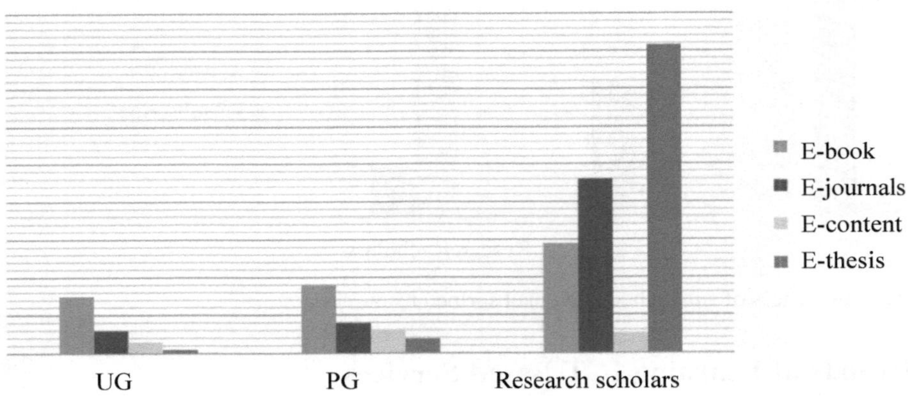

Graph 5.10. Type of e-resources access in central library

5.11 Purpose of Using ICT-based Services and E-resources

The graph 5.11 shows the purpose of using ICT-based services and e-resources among students of Kashi Vidyapith. It is observed that 45%of the UG students were used ICT-based services for preparing notes and assignments while 65%of the PG students were used ICT-based services for OPAC, preparing notes and assignments and article, etc. It is also observed that 85% of the research students use ICT-based services for prepare articles and theses, *etc.*

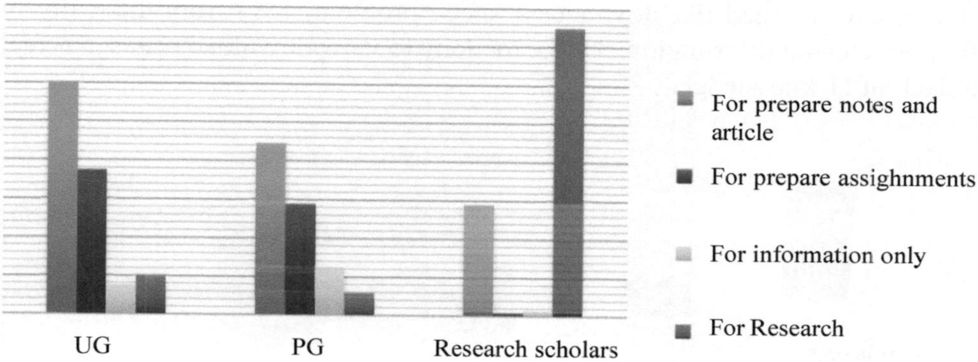

Graph 5.11. Type of e-resources Access in Central Library

5.12 Adequacy of ICT-Based Services and E-Resources

The graph 5.12 shows the Adequacy of ICT-based services and e-resources among students of Kashi Vidyapith. It is observed from the analysis that 55% of the UG students accept Adequacy of ICT-based services and e resources and 45% do not agree with this. While 62% of the PG students accept Adequacy of ICT-based services and e-resources and 38% do not agree with this. At research level, it is also observed that 80% of the research students are accept Adequacy of ICT-based services and e-resources and 20% do not agree with this.

Graph 5.12. Adequacy of ICT-based services and e-resources

5.13 Problems Faced while Using ICT-Based Services and E-Resources

The graph 5.13 shows the problems faced while using ICT-based services and E-resources among students of Kashi Vidyapith. It is observed that 62% of the students were faced the slow access speed problem, 15% from difficulty in finding relevant information. 8% for too long to view/download pages, 5% feel to lack of IT knowledge.

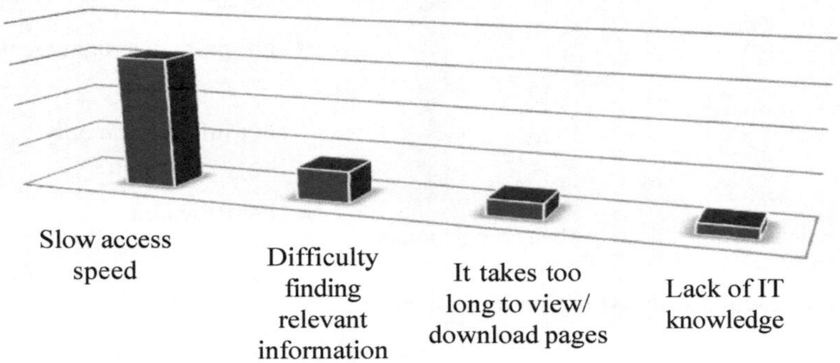

Graph 5.13. Problems faced while using ICT-based services and e resources

5.14 E-Resources versus Print Resources

The graph 5.14 shows the online services versus offline services among students of Kashi Vidyapith. It is observed that 45% of the students were in favor of offline and print services while 55% were in favor of online services and resources.

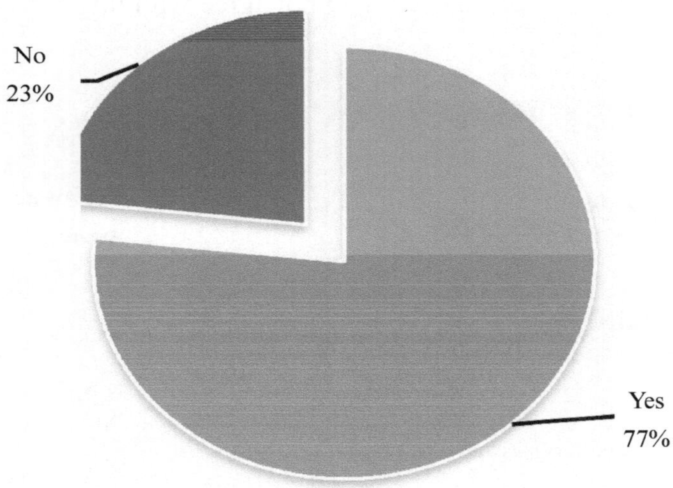

Graph 5.14. E-resources versus vs print resources

6. Conclusion

ICTSs are important and useful tools for achieving long-term development in all fields and aspects of our society. Globalization fueled by ICT is currently having a massive influence on library practices of Central Library Mahatma Gandhi Kashi Vidyapith. Since, ICTs practices are increasing but many of the students of the university preferred the print material. Mostly students use ICT-based services and e-resources of the central library by their laptop or mobile. ICTs, among other things, enable the achievement of developmental goals in library services. The use of ICT in the Central Library has resulted in providing traditional materials such as e-thesis, e-books, journals, newspapers and other library information resources to teachers, students and its users through ICT. The increase in ICT has also resulted in the creation of E-Library. Teachers, students and its users of Mahatma Gandhi Kashi Vidyapith can easily access current literature material using ICT. ICT-based library services during COVID-19 promote collaboration and collaboration among academics, and also provide library services to users who are remotely located in geographical locations.

References

Antherjanam, S.D., & Sheeja, N.K. (2008). Impact of ICT on library and information science: Major shifts and practices in CUSAT central library. In 6th International CALIBER-2008. University of Allahabad: Allahabad.

Bharati, V.K. (2018). E-Resources searching behavior of research scholars of Mahatma Gandhi Kashi Vidyapith, Varanasi: A case study, *Asian Journal of Information Science and Technology,* 8(1).

Cholin, V.S. (2005). Study of the application of information technology for effective access to resources in Indian University Libraries. *The International Information & Library Review*, 37(3).

MGKVP Central Library (2021). http://www.mgkvp.ac.in/library/lib_library profile.html MGKVP University (2021). http://www.mgkvp.ac.in/info/univ_university.html.

Obioha, J. (2005). The role of ICT in information seeking and use amongst research officers in research institutes in Nigeria: The Nigerian Institute for Oceanography & Marine Research Institute Experience. *The International Information & Library Review* 37(4).

Ramzan, M., & Singh, D. (2008). Status of information technology applications in Pakistani libraries. *The Electronic Library*, 27(4).

12

Use of Information Resources and Services by Faculty of Fashion Design Institute: A Study

Manjunatha S.R.[1] and Harish H.T.[2]

[1]*District Skill Development Office, Mandya, Karnataka – 571 401*

[2]*Sai Vidya Institute of Technology, Bengaluru, Karnataka – 560 064*

ABSTRACT

The study shows the use of information resources and services by the academia. Aim: study focuses on age, designation, gender, qualification and computer literacy impact all use of information resources and services. Objectives: To know the use of information resources by faculty of fashion institute, to study the awareness of OPAC among faculty of fashion institute, to find out the frequency of using library by faculty and to investigate the level of computer literacy. Methodology: used survey method, collected data through questionnaire method. The questionnaire designed and distributed 380 questionnaires to users of selected fashion design institute and we received 120 filled questionnaires. The outcome shows that they are satisfied with information resources and services of Fashion design institution.

Keywords: Information, Resources, Services, Fashion design, Fashion institution, Fashion technology, Swatch library; South India.

1. Introduction

Fashion is a general term for a currently current trends or practice, especially in clothing, foot wear or accessories. Fashion refers to anything that is the current trend in look and dress of a person. The more in general term "costume" which has been in popular use, has mostly been related to a special sense like fancy dress or masquerade wear, while the term "fashion" means clothing generally, and the study of it. For a broad cross-cultural look at clothing and its place in society, 'fashion' refers to the entries for clothing, costume and fabrics.

Today of fashion industry is a billion dollar industry. It is a huge umbrella of opportunities, growth and success. Principally concerned with clothing and lifestyle, this industry provides ample career opportunities for people from various cadres. Fashion industry is an unusual industry which blends creativity, art and technology for its emergence. This unique facet enables both creative techniques to be accommodated. Being a creative and glamour, oriented field, fashion industry perhaps witnesses most of the hardships to get a consignment done on dates or a ramp show to be a successful one. Unlike other industries this industry functions based on seasons. It is an industry which runs with the changing times and often undergoes changes in both manufacturing and retailing of products.

2. Review of Literature

Okike, B. I., & Oyeniyi, E. W. (2019). They opined that Information resources and services are considered valuable assets which are important in making right decisions. Information can fulfill this agenda only if it is delivered through effective reaching at the beneficiary's doorsteps. The growth of ICT, particular social media, has opened the doors in all productive sectors and service-oriented sectors such as libraries. The important need and use of social media by libraries for reaching out library users and make them to understand the myriad of safety implications that may exist. Bharathi, K., & Sujatha, H. R. (2019). Examined the utilization and effectiveness of digital libraries in 51 self-financed Engineering Colleges affiliated to the Visvesvaraya Technological University (VTU) in the Karnataka. They identified that digital resources maximum used by UG students to complete their project work. Through this we realize that a large extent among respondents with mean value of 2.28±0.89 use digital resources. The statistical test projected that there is a significant difference in utilization between student and faculty members as $p=0.000$. Sethy, J. K., & Jena, P. (2021). They explored usage of e- resources and services by NIFT, Bhubaneswar students and research scholar. Out of 130 questionnaires 101 filled questionnaires were use to do tabulation, analysis and interpretation of the data. How frequently they use e-resources and satisfaction level on using the same. The students and researcher were very much happy and satisfied with the use of e-resources. Mwaniki, P.W. (2018). Explains the role of college libraries in the era of new technology and user information needs and how staff should be equipped with new skills to give best services to the library users. The new technologies and the implications they have on the staff, library services and new user needs. The overall study targeted how to use new technology and provide library resources to the end users who use academic library. Its shows the future opportunities to librarians to advance their professional role. Pitla, Raja Suresh Kumar, *et al.* (2020). They made an attempt to know the use of e-resources in Krishna District (AP)

Engineering College Libraries. They distributed well designed questionnaires among 890 (Faculty) library users out of whom 705 responses were received representing 79% of the total sample. It is evident that 448 (63.54%) majority are male users, they found through this study that assistant professors 379 (53.75%) use library more, 259 (36.73%) faculty visit the library daily, 89.50 of faculty feel that library had convenient working hours to give best service to the library users. Faculty visit library to borrowing books, reference books and electronic journals in a maximum number. The majority of faculty use IEEE, SCOPUS, Springer, NPTEL e-resources and they are satisfied with IEEE, DELNET and NPTEL videos. With this they suggest that engineering college faculty are not aware of e-resources available in there library they need library orientation program from librarian. Choshaly, S. H., & Mirabolghasemi, M. (2019). They explained the impact of Libqual+™ dimension of services, information manage and Library as a spot) on satisfaction of library users at Universiti Kebangsaan Malaysia (UKM). Well designed questionnaire were distributed to 100 students and the same used to analysis by using SPSS and SmartPLS. They used composite consistency, convergent and distinguish validity was used to guess the relationships between variables. The impact of the study shows that services, information control and library as a spot have an important and optimistic impact on the overall satisfaction of users of Library, with affect of services being the most important role of library user satisfaction. Overall, students are happy with the services and facilities provided by the UKM library. This helped library professionals to make right decisions in giving right service to the right users in an effective way to fulfill the library users' needs, which matches with library vision and mission to make improvements and make library user satisfactory.

3. Objectives

1. To know the use of information resources by faculty of fashion institute.
2. To study the awareness of OPAC among faculty of fashion institute.
3. To find out the frequency of using library by faculty.
4. To investigate the level of computer literacy to use library resources by faculty of fashion institute.
5. To find out the satisfaction level with the library resources and services.

4. Scope and Limitation

The study target on use of information resources and services by faculty of fashion design institution and the scope of the study limited to institute libraries that are engaging in imparting undergraduate degree in the field of fashion design that too in Telangana, Karnataka, Kerala and Tamil Nadu.

5. Methodology

The investigator used survey method, collected data through questionnaire method. The questionnaire designed and distributed 380 questionnaires to users of selected fashion design institute and we received 120 filled questionnaires.

6. Result and Discussion

The investigator distributed a total of 380 questionnaires amongst the faculty of fashion design institution for the study, out of 380 questionnaires distributed a total 120 filled questionnaire were received. The details of the distribution analysis are described in table 6.1.

6.1. Designation wise Distribution

The designation of the faculty is taken as one of the variables for studying the use of information resources and services by faculty of fashion design institutes. The designation wise breakup of responses is shown in table 6.1 It observed from the table that majority of the respondents numbering 74(62%) are Assistant Professors, whereas 28 respondents representing 23 percent are Associate Professors and Professors represent 18 (15%).

Table 6.1: Designation

S/N	Designation	No of Responses	Percentage
1.	Professors	18	15
2.	Associate Professors	28	23
3.	Assistant Professors	74	62
	Total	**120**	**100**

6.2 Educational Qualifications

The qualification wise distribution shown in table 6.2 provides the details of the educational qualifications of the respondents. The M.Sc qualified respondents constituted the single largest category 39 (32.54%) of the sample. This was followed by the M.Tech and MBA qualified respondents who constituted 31 (25.83%) and 27 (22.5%) respectively. While the MA qualified respondents constituted 13 (10.8%) of the sample, those who were M.Phil and PhD qualified constituted 9 (7.5%) and 1 (0.83%) respectively in the study.

Table 6.2: Educational Qualifications

S/N	Educational Qualifications	No of Responses	Percentage
1.	MA	13	10.8
2.	MSc	39	32.54
3.	MBA	27	22.5
4.	M.Tech	31	25.83
5.	M.Phil	9	7.5
6.	Ph.D	1	0.83
	Total	**120**	**100**

6.3 Gender

The sample used for the study consisting of both male and female. The gender wise distribution of fashion design institutes faculty is shown in table 6.3 It may be seen from the table that majority of the respondents numbering 86 (72%) are female and the remaining 34 (28%) are male.

Table 6.3: Gender

S/N	Gender	No of Responses	Percentage
1.	Male	34	28
2.	Female	86	72
		Total	**120**

6.4 Age

Age made an important influence factor on the use of information resources and services in fashion design institute. It is assumed that higher the age, higher is the usage of information resources and services. But the researcher found that younger age (26-35) faculty use library information resources and services more than the senior and junior faculty members. The table 6.4 proved us that majority of the respondents numbering 64 (53.34%) are in the age group of 26 – 35 years. The respondents between the age group of 22-25 are 34 (28.33%) are the second largest. The last and the least one is above 36 that is 22(18.33%) of respondents. The table clearly shows that users in the age group between 26 – 35 are the highest.

Table 6.4: Age

S/N	Range of Age	No. of Responses	Percentage
1.	22-25 yrs	34	28.33
2.	26- 35	64	53.34
3.	> 36 yrs	22	18.33
	Total	**120**	**100**

6.5 How Frequently do you Visit Library

How frequently faculty of fashion design institute visit library is showcased in table 6.5 and table shows that who visited library twice in a week constituted the single largest category 64 (53.33%) of the sample. Those doing so thrice in a week followed at 40 (33.33%). The faculty of fashion design institute visiting library daily and rarely constituted 11(9.16%) and 5(2.87%) respectively.

Table 6.5: How frequently do you visit library

S/N	Frequency	No of Respondents	Percentage
1.	Daily	11	9.16
2.	Twice in week	64	53.33
3.	Thrice in week	40	34.64
4.	Rarely	5	2.87
	Total	**120**	**100.0**

6.6 Level of Computer Literacy

The computer literacy shown in table 6.6 provides the details of the Computer literacy of the respondents. 65 respondents that is 54.17% have good computer literacy, 37 respondents are expert in computer literacy that is 30.83% and remaining 18 respondents having average computer literacy that is 15%.

Table 6.6: Level of Computer literacy

S/N	Frequency	No of Respondents	Percentage
1.	Excellent	37	30.83
2.	Good	65	54.17
3.	Average	18	15
	Total	**120**	**100**

6.7 Awareness About OPAC (Online Public Access Catalogue)

Awareness of OPAC (Online Public Access Catalogue) is mentioned in table 6.9 It may be seen from the below table that majority of the respondents that is 53(52.40%) are not aware of OPAC (Online Public Access Catalogue). Remaining 67 (47.60%) are having awareness of OPAC (Online Public Access Catalogue).

Table 6.7: Awareness of OPAC (Online Public Access Catalogue)

S/N	Type of response	No of Responses	Percentage
1	Yes	67	47.60
2	No	53	52.40
	Total	**120**	**100.0**

6.8 Mode of Awareness of OPAC (Online Public Access Catalogue)

The Mode of awareness of OPAC (Online Public Access Catalogue) is presented in table 6.8 that there are several sources with which the faculty becomes aware the availability of OPAC (Online Public Access Catalogue). Out of 120 respondents scoring 80 (66.68%) of the total respondents learnt about OPAC (Online Public Access Catalogue) from 'Librarian, about 38 respondents scoring 31.66%, approached 'Library professional staff' to know about OPAC (Online Public Access Catalogue) and the remaining least percentage 2 (1.66%) of respondents learnt from Colleagues.

Table 6.8: Mode of awareness of OPAC (Online Public Access Catalogue)

S/N	Mode of Awareness	No of Responses	Percentage
1	Librarian	80	66.68
2	Library professional staff	38	31.66
3	Colleagues	2	1.66
	Total	**120**	**100.0**

6.9 Awareness About Swatch library

Awareness of Swatch library is highlight in table 6.9 It may be seen from the below table that majority of faculty 88(73.34%) are aware of Swatch library remaining 32 (26.66%) faculty are not aware of Swatch library.

Table 6.9: Awareness about Swatch library

S/N	Type of Response	No of Responses	Percentage
1	Yes	88	73.34
2	No	32	26.66
	Total	**120**	**100**

6.10 Purpose of Using Swatch Library

An attempt was made here to find out the Purpose of using Swatch library by faculty of fashion design institute is shown in table 6.10 It may be seen from the table that maximum number of faculty that is 112 (93.34%) use Swatch Library to teach practical's followed by 8 respondents scoring 6.66% who use for others.

Table 6.10: Purpose of using Swatch library

S/N	Type of Response	No of Responses	Percentage
1	To teach practical	112	93.34
2	Project	0	0
3	To prepare class	0	0
4	Other	8	6.66
	Total	**120**	**100**

6.11 Purpose of Using Library Resources

This show about purpose of using library resources showed in the table 6.11 for the four attributes.' 'To know recent trends in fashion field' has the highest percentage of 75 (62.5%) respondents are to some extent followed by 'Research' has the highest percentage of 57 (47.5%) respondents are to great extent, followed by 'Education' has the highest percentage of 54 (45) respondents are to a some. It clearly shows that 'to know recent trends in fashion field' has the highest percentage of 75 (62.5.5) respondents are to a great extent.

Table 6.11: Purpose of Using Library Resources

S/N	Attributes	Responses in Percentage (N=120)				
		1	2	3	4	5
1.	Research	0	0	7 (5.84)	56 (46.66)	**57 (47.5)**
2.	Teaching	10(8.33)	0	4 (3.34)	**54 (45)**	52 (43.33)
3.	To know recent trends in fashion field	0	0	4 (3.34)	**75 (62.5)**	41(34.16)

Note: 1- Strongly disagree, 2- Disagree, 3- Neither agree nor disagree, 4- Agree, 5- Strongly agree.

6.12: Satisfied with the Library Resource and Services

Southern states of Indian fashion design institute faculty attitude about the Satisfaction by using information resources and services is shown in the table 6.12 that majority of respondents 84 (70%) are satisfied with library resources and services remaining not satisfied with information resources and services provide by the fashion design institute library that is 36 (30%).

Table 6.12: Satisfied with the library resource and services

S/N	Satisfied with the library resource and services	No of Responses	Percentage
1	Yes	84	70
2	No	36	30
	Total	**120**	**100**

7. Summary

- Majority of the respondents numbering 86 (72%) are female
- Study found that younger age (26-35) faculty use library information resources and services more than the senior and junior faculty members.
- Majority of the respondents visited library twice in a week.
- 66.68% of the total respondents learnt about OPAC (Online Public Access Catalogue) from Librarian.
- Majority of faculty 88(73.34%) are aware of Swatch library.
- Maximum number of faculty that is 112 (93.34%) uses Swatch Library to teach practical.
- Majority of the respondents use resources to know recent trends in fashion field has the highest percentage of 75 (62.5%).
- Majority of respondents 84 (70%) are satisfied with library resources and services.

8. Conclusion

Today with the opening of information and communication technology the learning resource environment has changed a lot. Faculty of Fashion Design Institute moving towards right direction and the same proved in the study that faculty has positive attitude about Information resources and services and they are satisfied by using it for their academic needs.

References

Arpita, Khare (2014). How cosmopolitan are Indian consumers?: A study on fashion clothing involvement. *Journal of Fashion Marketing and Management*, 18(4), 431–451.

Claire Warwick *et al.* (2008). Library and information resources and users of digital resources in the humanities. *Program: electronic library and information systems,* 42(1), 5–27.

Devendra Kumar, & Rajkumar Singh (2009). Information resources and services of national science library India, New Delhi: A user study. *International Journal of Library and Information Science,* 1(2), 17–21.

Marguerite A., Nel, & Ina Fourie (2016). Information behaviour and expectations of veterinary researchers and their requirements for academic library services. *The Journal of Academic Librarianship,* 42(1), 44–54.

13

Relevancy of H-Index in the Digital World: A Primordial Approach

Renu

Department of Library & Information Science, Maharshi Dayanand University Rohtak, Haryana – 124 001

ABSTRACT

Nowadays it is very important to evaluate research publications. They are evaluated by impact factors and citation indices. The research value of an author and journal is ascertained from several citation indices, from which it is known that what Impact of a research publication is in market. The h index is based on diagnostic importance or productivity so it confers a delegate index of scientific result. The h-index is used to measure of published work of a scientist or scholar as well as also assess the achievement of research groups. The present paper describe about the h-index. Specifically, it explains its origin, advantages, and disadvantages and how calculates individual's h-index in different databases.

Keywords: Citation, Impact, H-Index, Research productivity, Scientific publications.

1. Introduction

The h-index is determined by the number of citations received by a researcher for his or her works. It takes into account the total number of publications as well as the number of citations per publication. The h-index seeks to assess a scientist's or scholar's production as well as the effect of their published work. The index is based on a set of a scientist's most cited works as well as the number of other publications in which they have been cited. In assessing the scientific effect of individual researchers' or research centers' work, the h-index is an alternative to more typical journal impact factor measurements. As citations accrue, the h-index rises; the most frequently cited publications contribute to the h-index. "The h-index can be manually determined using citation databases or using automatic tools and available calculators (*e.g.*, in Scopus and Web of Knowledge databases). Harzing's Publish or Perish program provides h-indices calculated using Google Scholar entries" (Horzyk, n.d.). The journal

Chemistry World, published by the Royal Society of Chemistry, in the UK, decided to stop publishing an online ranking that was popular with readers. It was the list-updated a few times a year-of more than 500 highly productive researchers in the field of chemistry, those whose h-index was greater than 55. The decision to halt the ranking was made in response to complaints that it placed too much focus on a single performance metric, ignoring other factors of scientific productivity, and could lead institutions and funding organisations to make rash or questionable judgments. The largest number "h" of his or her research articles with at least the same number "h" of citations is defined as a researcher's h-index. With an h-index of 169, Harvard University's George Whitesides was the highest-ranked author in Chemistry World. This is the same as claiming he published at least 169 articles, each of which received at least 169 citations in other works. You must publish publications that have an impact on the scientific community in order to achieve a high h-index. A researcher's h-index will be low if she publishes a lot but is rarely quoted, or if she receives a lot of citations but only produces a few publications.

2. Origin of H-index

In 2005, Argentinean physicist Jorge Hirsch, a professor at the University of California, San Diego, proposed the h-index as a measure for assessing the quantity and quality of scholarly articles. It quickly became a metric used in evaluations and on the business cards of top researchers, and it's now being used to gauge the performance of groups of academics, universities, countries, and publications. The criticism began with the inaugural edition of the rankings in 2007 and has never stopped, according to Henry Schaefer, professor at the University of Georgia in Athens and the person responsible for generating the Chemistry World list. "The problem was not with the h-index itself, but with the ranking that placed too much emphasis on this indicator," he explained. Jorge E. Hirsch of UCSD published this study in PNAS in 2005, proposing the h-index as a tool for assessing and comparing individual scientists' total research production. Many committees and bodies have immediately chosen the h-index as their preferred metric. The h-index is a straight forward concept. Do you, for example, have at least one paper that has been cited? If you answered yes, you can move on to the next step in the process. Have each of your two papers been cited twice? If you answered yes, your h-index must be at least two. You can continue till you reach a "no." So, if your h-index is 20, it signifies you've published 20 papers with at least 20 citations. It also suggests you're doing quite well in your studies! Hirsch believes that a h index of 20 is good, 40 is great, and 60 is genuinely exceptional after 20 years of research.

3. Definition of H-index

"An index that quantifies both the actual scientific productivity and the apparent scientific impact of a scientist." e.g. A researcher with an h-index of 25 has 25 articles, each of which has been cited 25 times or more. Physicist Jorge Hirsch proposed the h-index as a comparative assessment of an individual's scientific effect.

"Hirsch states simply that the h-index is an indicator of the impact of a researcher on the development of his or her scientific field" (Hirsch and Buela-Casal, 2014, p. 163).

The h-index was proposed by J.E. Hirsch in his paper "An index to quantify an individual's scientific research output".

4. Calculate their H-index in Different Databases

The h-index is a metric for determining the influence of a researcher's work based on how many times that researcher's work has been cited. You may easily determine a scientist's h-index using many web services. The most well-known are ISI Web of Knowledge and Scopus, which both cost a subscription (most likely through your institute), but there are several free options, such as Publish or Perish. You might obtain a different value if you check your own (or someone else's) h-index with each of these databases. This is because each counts total publications and citations using a different database. Publish or perish uses Google Scholar, while ISI and Scopus use their own databases. Because each database has a varied coverage, the h-index values will differ. For example, ISI has good journal coverage but low conference coverage, whereas Scopus has higher conference coverage but poor journal coverage prior to 1992. The h-index is a valuable indicator for measuring scientific performance, but only in conjunction with other parameters. So, while making crucial decisions (financing, job, choosing a PI), check the publication list, chat to other scientists (and students) and peers, and consider your career stage. So, keep in mind that while an h-index is one factor among many—and you should certainly know yours—it does not define you (or anybody else) as a scientist. Because both Web of Science and Google Scholar can track citations, they can be used to compute a researcher's h-index. While Web of Science and Google Scholar will compute an h-index for you, knowing how to do it manually is very useful. The h-index is derived by finding all published papers in a certain database (such as Web of Science or Google Scholar) and sorting them by number of citations in descending order.

5. Age Factor is Important in the H-index

A scientist's h-index rises steadily with time, and the trend is roughly linear, according to empirical evidence. In reality, theoretical reasoning in my original study suggested that the h-index increases linearly with scientists' "scientific age" (i.e., the time from their first publication), whereas the overall number of citations increases quadratically. As a result, I proposed the m index (the quotient of the h-index divided by the number of years from the scientist's first publication) as a "timeless" measure for comparing scientists at various phases in their careers (Hirsch & Buela-casal, 2014). The h-index cannot be used to compare researchers at different phases of their careers—a senior chemist with an h-index of 100 can be pleased of her high productivity, but so can a young chemist with an h-index of 30. Comparing the results of researchers from different fields is also misleading. According to Rogério Meneghini, scientific coordinator of the SciELO Brazil library, each topic has its own size and citation trends. The number of researchers in biochemistry, for example, is enormous. As a result, more papers are being published, and more individuals are citing articles. When conducting comparisons, the rule is to look at sub-areas, according to Meneghini, who thinks the h-index is a useful tool, especially in the natural sciences. "A high h-index in these areas is a sign that the researcher did important research," he says.

6. How does the Language of Publication Influence the H-index?

The "universal" scientific language is English. As a result, publications written in English are inevitably cited more than papers written in other languages, such as Spanish. This translates to lower h-indices for scientists who publish in these other languages. I've occasionally come across intriguing papers written in languages I don't understand, such as Russian, and have had them translated and referenced. On other times, though, I have found it more convenient to use equivalent English-language publications that were not as good but were easier to find.

7. Disadvantages of the H-Index

Hirsch created the h-index to overcome the major flaws in other bibliometric metrics like total number of papers or total number of citations. He asserted that the total number of papers does not reflect the quality of scientific publications, but that participation in a single influential publication can have a disproportionate impact on the total number of citations. A higher number of citations can be generated by low-quality methodological papers offering new procedures or methods than by high-quality publications. The h-index is designed to assess both the quality and quantity of scientific output at the same time. There is much misleading information about a scientist's output and the drawbacks of using the h-index to evaluate and compare the achievements of individual scientists, research groups, institutions, or countries. and some disadvantages are:

- It does not take the number of authors on a manuscript into consideration. A scientist who is the sole author of a publication with 100 citations should be given more credit than a scientist who is one of ten co-authors on a similarly referenced paper.
- It penalises scientists who are just starting out in their careers. Even if all of their papers are ground breaking and widely cited, outstanding scientists with a modest number of publications cannot have a high h-index. For example, if "Albert Einstein died in early 1906, then his *h*-index would be stuck at 4 or 5, despite his being widely acknowledged as one of the most important physicists, even considering only his publications to that date."
- Because review articles are cited more frequently than original publications, they have a bigger impact on the h-index.

8. Conclusion

The h-index should lead to better decisions on scientific employment and promotion, awarding of prizes, and membership in honorary societies. Allocation of research funding by government agencies must choose between competing proposals. As long as this index is well-used, I believe it will contribute favorably to scientific advancement and assist to fairly reward people who contribute to it.

References

Hirsch, J. E., & Buela-casal, G. (2014). The meaning of the h-index. *International Journal Of Clinical and Health Psychology*, 14(2), 161–164. http://doi.org/10.1016/S1697-2600 (14) 70050-X

https://library.ucar.edu/finding-your-h-index-hirsch-index-web-science

https://bitesizebio.com/13614/does-your-h-index-measure-up/

https://libguides.bc.edu/articleinfluence/hindex

http://leddy.uwindsor.ca/impact-h-index-web-science-and-google-scholar

http://revistapesquisa.fapesp.br/en/2013/06/25/the-limits-of-the-h-index/

14

Electronic Resource Management Issues and Concerns

Geetu Bala

Chandigarh College of Architecture, Chandigarh – 160 012

ABSTRACT

This paper discusses the various issues and concerns about the electronic information resources, which includes mainly such as e-journals, e-books and e-databases *etc*. In this digital era, the library should be well equipped with trendy facilities & resources within the sort of books, manuscripts, technical journals, standards, conference proceedings, theses, reports, databases, and all the electronic versions of information resources. Various issues and concerns, which are related with the electronic resources and their management is discussed in detailed in this paper.

Keywords: ICT, Electronic resources, e-journals, Electronic resource management.

1. Introduction

This the era of Information and Communication Technology (ICT) and every walk of human life has been widely affected. Traditional ways and means of working has now totally been replaced by the ICT based innovations. Academic institutions are widely affected by the ICT and its implementation in teaching and learning process. Similarly, the libraries have to force to change its type of resources and services as per the demands of the users. A library is termed as the heart of any organization. The traditional libraries have comprised mainly of printed materials like books, periodicals, magazines, newspapers and some libraries have non-conventional documents such as atlas, manuscripts, maps, cassettes, audio-video, films, *etc*. But with the increase development in information and communication technologies, modern libraries are evolving worldwide. Nowadays, most of the information and resources are available in electronic form, which are easy to procure, use and edit. Providing access rather than holding electronic resources in libraries are currently getting a great deal of attention. Libraries are trying to make accessible information embedded in electronic resources to fulfill various information needs of the users.

Due to many benefits, electronic form of information and resources now became popular choice of the readers. Electronic resources can easily be accessible from anywhere, anytime, and as per the convenience of individual. Every organization has now turned its activities digitally and tries to procure all the documents and information in digital form. The e-resources are made available both online and offline. Furthermore, some are freely available and some are paid. The free e-resources can be accessed anywhere and anytime on the discretion of the user, whereas, for the paid e-resources to get comprehensive access by using best possible tools and techniques is the library.

The management of digital resources has never been an easy process. The rapid expansion of digital resources compounded with changing formats and sales models in the short life of web-based delivery systems has particularly made the management process more complex. Furthermore, from the very beginning, details relating to purchasing, subscription, licenses, access, annual maintenance charges (AMCs), if any, and usage have been kept in the system adopted or followed by the library or librarian.

2. Factors Influencing in Electronic Era

New technologies are taking place at every stage. Technological advances always bring revolution in all disciplines. Some of the factors, which reflecting all the human endeavors are as follows.

2.1. Augmentation of ICT

From many of the subjects, science is the recent development in information communication and technology. The speed, at which new ICT techniques are emerging, is mind-boggling. Information communication and technologies has triggered a change in the ways in which the information is created, stored, retrieved and disseminated. Library professionals are readily adopting new technologies in order to make access to information resources easier for the users.

2.2. Emergence of Internet

The networks and networking technology is the beauty of ICT, which shrinks the physical boundaries and makes the world a global village. A combination of advances in computers and network protocols has helped to create Internet. It is an interconnection of large and small networks around the globe. Internet is used in every sphere of life and access is being universal. The www is a hypertext system built on top of Internet. It is a client server-based distribution hypertext multimedia information system. Web browsers allow users to easily browse through tens of thousands of sites around the world. Jagtar Singh (2002) observed that "the high-speed networks have an immense potential to provide real-time access to vast amounts of networked information. Internet has emerged as the world's largest repository of information". Information sources available through the networks such as the Internet and Bitnet have proliferated and diversified in recent years.

2.3. Electronic Publishing

Lancaster (1989) defined electronic publishing as a "Publishing process where the documents are submitted in electronic format, edited, printed to subscribers and readers by employing computers and telecommunications. In general it could be understood that the word Publication literally means making public and word Electronic refers to information that is stored in computer. Material is produced electronically may be classified into two categories one is communication and second is information management. Electronic publishing in simple words can be explained as a method which involves ICT and publishing technology to deliver created information to the users in the form of non-print media usually through electronic networks such as Internet and local area networks. Earlier it was thought that the Internet is not a forum for serious publishing, and the scientific credits researchers gain by these publications are not equal to scientific publications proper. Electronic publishing has emerged as transforming technology to libraries because it is making available information in electronic format on the web and more and more information is being generated in this format independent from time and space constraints. The concept of easy access to information in electronic format is converting many dreams into realities. Electronic publishing has led to a new era of information communication and sharing in the form of electronic library.

3. Electronic Resources

In most simple words, when we process data and convert it into meaningful and useful form, it becomes information, when this information is fetch in electronic form it is called electronic resources.

3.1. Journals

Electronic journals are used for those journals and newsletters that are equipped and distributed electronically. Today the electronic resources are covering books, magazines, theses, newspapers and bibliographic databases. Electronic journals or e-journals are an invaluable source of up to date scholarly information.

3.2. Magazines

Magazine (e-magazines), also called periodical, a printed or digitally published collection of texts (essays, articles, stories, poems).

3.3. Encyclopedia

Encyclopedia is a set of books that gives vast information about many subjects, arranged in the order of the alphabet from A-Z. For example, every library has a set of Encyclopedia Britannia and Encyclopedia Americana. Now, encyclopedias are available in electronic form.

3.4. Newspapers

Newspaper, that provides news, views, features, and other information of public interest. It is publishing daily basis and every library has the subscription of newspaper for their student and researchers. In this Internet era, now newspapers are available in online form and anyone can also be able to download in pdf form as well.

4. Types of Electronic Resources

Electronic resources are available in the following types.

4.1. Direct Access Resources

They are basically two types of electronic resources and can be used at any time. These have two sub-types.

- **Static e-resources:** Static e-resources are those documents, which contains fixed information and never change their form, for example, the traditional online data.
- **Dynamic e-resources:** Dynamic e-resources are those documents, which contains fixed information but they are able to change their form, for example, multimedia, CD-ROM.

4.2. Indirect Access Resources

Some e-resources are accessed indirectly such as consortium based e-resources. In this cutting throat competition and shrinking budget, none of the library fulfill the informational requirements of the users so libraries would like to be a part of consortium so that their users can also access the contents freely. Some of the examples of the consortiums are UGC-Infonet and CeRA (Consortium for e-Resources in Agriculture).

5. Access Models to E-journals

Electronic resources are suitable to use and access information from the library, Internet café, office and home. There are some models for accessing the e-resources as follows.

- **Remote access:** In this model, vendors/publishers host their journals at their websites. When an individual institution of organization or a library subscribes to their e-journals, they are provided the rights to access the contents.
- **IP enabled (Intranet)**: This method can be used by the libraries which have Intranet based LAN in their libraries or campus. In this method the publisher's server site validate the IP address of user's Intranet server whenever a user logs into the publisher's website for a subscribed journal to access the contents.
- **Combined**: Every publisher have different method for provide the access of e-journals. Some publishers offer a combination of both the above models. This issue is largely decided by the publisher's policy of how much access is to be provided.
- **On site access:** In this model, the library can host the e-journals within its LAN (Local Area Network).
- **User-ID and Password:** In this model the subscriber gets a user-ID and password, which can be used from any user terminal in the Institution/ library, largely constrained to one immediate user at a time.
- **Access through database:** Some publishers have been producing their contents in an electronic format for years. Access models accessible by publishers limit the access to their journals, but the users regularly find articles of their interest through the databases.

6. Advantages of E-resources

E- Resources have many advantages, some of these advantages are:

- First of all, Internet connectivity is must, without Internet connectivity we can't access e-resources. The users need not physically visit the library. This is very useful for the users.
- E-resources have multi user access.

- E-resources are having 24 x 7 access, means users can access the e-resources anytime.
- It is (Electronic version) available before print version is coming out.
- Provided timely access to the documents.
- Support different searching capabilities.
- It is available with the print version is published above the Internet.
- The readers can search a large number of e-resources.
- E-resources are easy to use.
- E-resources also provide usage figures means library staff can find-out which journals or magazine is popular among the users.
- Space is the big problem of every library and the procuring e-resources helps libraries in resolving the issue of space.

7. Disadvantages of E-resources

- The readers need to have access to Internet in order to read electronic resources.
- Without Internet connectivity you cannot access the e-resources.
- Initial high cost expenditure on infrastructure & installation of physical instruments.
- Need of special equipments to access the e-contents.
- Difficulty in continuous viewing of data on screen.
- Copyright issues
- Renewal is must for the subscription on annual basis on most of the cases.
- We have to give training for library professionals and users to access the e-resources.
- Plagiarism issues.
- Pricing issues.
- Security problems.
- Problems in going through the articles on the computer screen as it is very much scrupulous job to read the articles on computer screen.

8. Electronic Resource Management (ERM)

The management of electronic resources has never been an easy process. The role of management of electronic resources is to provide the right information to the right user at right time in the right manner. The management of print document is very easy for libraries but the management of e-resources is very complex. Generally, it seems that some libraries are not properly aware of issues related to management of electronic resources like collection development, analyzing user needs, orientation and training program for staff and user. Electronic Resource Management (ERM) is a term that refers to the practice of managing electronic data.

The electronic resources are altogether differing than that of traditional sources of information in the library. The concept of Electronic resources management can be clarified as a set of procedures that collects, processes, stores and disseminates the information to help and coordinate the activities of decision-making to remove insecurity. The steps required for managing e-resources are more complex than those for print resources. Electronic resources are a time-intensive process, often requiring more staff with a greater skill set at each stage.

For an effective search of appropriate literature the present library software have not adequate provision. In order to satisfy the user needs effectively, Electronic Resource Management (ERM) is required. ERM services are a way of thinking about library management to help libraries optimize the access, usage, data, and workflows of electronic library collections in the physical and digital library. Electronic resources, particularly e-journals and e-books, can be viewed as an integral part of library collections. Recent studies have shown that not only are libraries acquiring significant amounts of digital contents but also it also replacing and eclipsing traditional media. For this, some libraries have developed their own local system and some have procured the commercial ERM software.

9. Training for Users and Staff

Constant training is mandatory in the new information environment. All the staff members need to be concerned. The libraries may provide Internet connectivity and dial-up access to all its users' is that they can access the subscribed electronic resources. Improve information seeking skills of users supported by self teaching tutorials and outline help desks. Manpower is must for the smooth functioning of library. Human resources are the key to the successful use of any Information Technology in the library. The participation of the library staff is necessary for effective use of e-journals. Training programs act as a bridge to ease communication amongst members and find answers to common problems. Library staff members must be deputed to provide support to the library users with new e-journals facilities so that users can use the e-journals independently without much help from the library staff again and again.

10. Organization of Electronic Eesources

Organization involves the illustration, organization and storage of electronic resources and access to it. General principles of organization of print resources are applicable to organize and access electronic resources. It is necessary to organize e-resources keeping in view the priorities and availability of specific institutions and users.

11. Processing of E-resources

Today every library is trying to procure information resources which are available in electronic format so proper processing of acquired electronic resources is must for proper information retrieval.

12. Archiving

The process of maintaining the electronic resources in a condition suitable for use and the continued ability to render or display the content is called Archiving. The acquired and processed electronic resources are archived for further retrieval of right information to right user. The electronic resources such as disks, magnetic tapes, floppies, digital video disks and audio-visual aids used through help of computers are to be maintained and shelved properly. The electronic resources can also suffer from ghosting, if not used regularly. So every library has to take care in archival of e-resources properly.

13. Dissemination

Dissemination is the stage in which the electronic resources are accessible to the user. Dissemination activities can be performed by publicity material like brochures, awareness programmes, presentations at seminars and conferences, hosting a web site. This will help the users to know the existence of electronic resources for the electronic resources better and effective utilization. If a library able to procure and archive e-resources properly, than information could be disseminated effectively as well as up to the satisfaction level of the users.

14. Technologies Required for Electronic Resources

Unlike print resources, decisions regarding acquisition of electronic resources are indirectly dependent upon the availability of suitable technology. Electronic resources are machine dependent. Electronic resources management require possession of certain specific technologies like storage technologies- a variety of devices to store and retrieve information in electronic form such as magnetic tapes/cassettes, floppy disks, hard disks. Not only is the availability of computers, in the libraries, to access electronic resources but also the electronic resources design important. Some of the technological requirements for electronic resources are.

- **Audio visual**: Color T.V., V.C.R., D.V.D., Sound box, Telephone, *etc.*
- **Computer**: Server, P.C. with multimedia, U.P.S., *etc.*
- **Network**: LAN, MAN, WAN, Internet, *etc.*
- **Printer**: Laser printer, Dot matrix, Barcode printer, Digital graphic printer, *etc.*
- **Storage dévices**: Optical Storage Device, CD-ROM, *etc.*

15. Future Aspect of Electronic Resources

In the changing times, libraries and librarians will have to play a crucial role in handling electronic resources. The final goal of electronic publishing is to provide fast & easy access to the information contained in the objective publications with simple, controlling search and retrieval capabilities. So today's libraries have not just remain as the traditional libraries, rather they have urbanized into an Information Centers which are collecting, organizing electronic learning resources/ digital objects to provide access to the end users. Many libraries are currently experiencing a fast change from print to electronic format while developing collection of an Academic, Technical/ Special Libraries. The Internet has given rise to the development of electronic versions of printed library reading materials like books, journals, report, conference proceedings.

16. Challenges for Managing Electronic Resources

Some of the issues and challenges, which are commonly facing during managing the e-resources are as follows.

- Needs continuous up gradation in ICT infrastructure
- Inadequate financial support from the parent organizations
- Lack of cooperation from the staff members
- Preservation issues
- Copyrights and Digital Rights Management (DRM) issues
- Needs changes in collection development policies and guidelines
- Storage / Archiving of E-resources for future usage
- The main challenge is to clarify what is meant exactly by e-resource.

17. Conclusion

Electronic resources are the emerging source of information for all types of users in every organization. Today Internet being established as a key medium for the publication of information so libraries and information centers are taking responsibility for preserving online material. However, e-resources create challenges in every level of selection, acquisition, preservation, maintenance and management. In spite of the challenges, e-resources become popular due to its many advantages and above all easy to search and use. The e-resources are able to keep the researchers up to date and save their search time. So e-resources are beneficial to the users. Therefore, for proper e-resources management, more cooperation and interaction are required among library professionals, publishers, vendors/aggregators, users and software engineers to discuss common issues to arrive at common goal of mutual interests to promote more production, use of these resources with their improved, maintenance and management to the maximum benefit of the users. So electronic resources are easy to generate, edit, store, retrieve and use but due to some technical and logical issues management of electronic resources is a challengeable task.

References

Adika, G. (2003). Internet user among faculty members of University in Ghana. *Library Review*, 52(1), 29-37.

Arms, W. (2000). *Digital Libraries*. Cambridge, MA: MIT Press.

Arora, J. (2000). *Electronic publishing: An overview. Presented in National Seminar on Knowledge Networking in Engineering & Technology Education and Research.* New Delhi: IIT Delhi.

Breaks, M. (1999). Management of electronic information. *http://educate.lib.chalmers.se/IATUL/proceedcontents/chanpap/breaks.html*

Chohda, Nirupma (2015). Use of e-resources in Panjab University Library, Chandigarh. *International Journal of Digital Library Services*, 5(4), 54–61.

Dadzie, P. S. (2005). Electronic resources: access and usage at Ashesi University College. *Campus-Wide Information Systems*, 22(5), 290-297.

Dhingra, Navjyoti, & Mahajan, Preeti (2012). Electronic journal in the university libraries of Punjab: the present situation and future perspective. *International Journal of Digital Library Services*, *2*(1), 53-69.

Dhingra, Navjyoti, & Vasishta, Seema (2007). *E-journals: problem or panacea for higher Education.* Presented at UGC sponsored National Seminar on *Managing College Libraries in the Digital Environment: Opportunities and Challenges* at Dev Samaj College for Women, Chandigarh, India (pp. 94-101), 3-4 August 2007. http://eprints.rclis.org/16702/2/ journals_ Problem_ or_Panacea_for_Higher _Education.pdf.

Electronic Resources (2009.). *Electronic resources.* http://www.loc.gov/acq/devpol/electron.html

Fan, K. (2003). Electronic resources for Chinese studies and East Asian libraries. *New Library World*, 104(1093), 404-411.

Glossary and reference book (2010). *Harrod's Librarians Glossery*. http://lisdpt. community. officelive.com/Documents/HarrodLibrariansGlossary.pdf

Lancaster, F. (1995). The evolution of electronic publishing. *Library Trends*, 43(4), 518-527.

Majumdar, A., & Deka, D. (2008). *Access of e-resources by the users of LNB Library with special reference to UGC-Infonet: An Evaluative Survey 6th Convention PLANNER*, November 06-07. Nagaland: University Nagaland.

National Library of Australia (2008). *National Library of Australia, Canberra.* www.nla.gov.au/initiativis/meeting/sitelicens/sitlic.

Nisonger, T. (1997). E.J. collection management issues. *Collection Building*, 16(2), 58-65. https://www.nios.ac.in/media/documents/SrSecLibrary/LCh-008.pdf

Sathyanarayana, N.V. (2000). Electronic journals: access and delivery models. *DRTC annual seminar of Electronic Sources of information,* 1-3 March, 2000.

Seema, S. (2019). Changing trends of collection development for 21st century at Panjab University Library, Chandigarh: a move towards e-resource. *International Journal of Library Information Network*, 4(2), 122–132.

Sinha, M. K. (2015). Electronic Resource Management in University and Institutional Libraries of India in Changing Environments: An Overview.

Vasishta, S. (2007). Electronic information resources management. *The New Alley. In book entitled Libraries in Digital Environment: Problems and Prospects edited by Sunil Kumar Satpathy, Chandrakant Swain, Bijayalaxmi Rautaray.* Mahamaya Publishing House, New Delhi, 81-94.

Vasishta, S. (2008.). Networked Electronic Information Resources (NEIR). *Society at Deptt. of Some Instructive Thoughts. Presented at ICSSR sponsored Seminar on Trends and Strategic Issues for Libraries in Global Information society at Deptt. of Library & Information Sc, 18-19.* Chandigarh: Punjab University, 399-404. http://eprints.rclis.org/16688/2/Networked_Electronic_Information_Resources.pdf

Vasishta, S., & Kalra, H. (2009). Electronic journal access at PEC University of Technology Library: *A case study of managing technology and change. Paper published in proceedings of the 12th National Convention on Knowledge, Library and Information Networking (NACLIN-2009) on Managing Knowledge, Technology and Change in Libraries* (pp. 22-25 sept). Chandigarh: Punjab University.

Vasishta, Seema, & Dhingra, Navjyoti (2007). *Harnessing electronic information resources through prospective consortia approach: a national necessity, In Recent Trends in Library and information Science (RTLIS-07)*, NIT Hamirpur, Himachal Pradesh, India, 15-16 November 2007. 234-240. http://eprints.rclis.org/16686/5/Harnessing_Electronic_ Information_Resources_through_Prospective_Consortia_Approach.pdf.

15

Library Services & Assistive Technologies to Persons with Hearing Impairment

Amit Kumar

Punjab Agricultural University, Ludhiana – 141 004, Punjab

ABSTRACT

The hearing impaired Persons constitute a very small percentage of the total population. The article presents the information regarding the infrastructure, the library services to the special group of library users. All the public/academic libraries do not provide services to these groups of the users, hence the institutions specially meant for these persons are responsible for administering services to this group of users. Assistive technology can help to a great extent in providing library services to these groups of users.

***Keywords**:* Physically challenged persons, Hearing impaired library users, Library infrastructure, Library services, Information Technology, Assistive devices.

1. Introduction

The basic function of the library is to satisfy the intellectual needs of the readers. The libraries play important role in the lives of the persons with hearing disability. Library is a social institution and must be planned and organized according to social needs *i.e.* the actual and potential needs the community. It is also expected to serve the community of special type of users. In setting up a library for these users, certain basic factors are to be considered. It is apparently clear that these persons are in need of library for various kinds of services, which are routinely available to the normal people.

2. Physically Challenged Persons

Generally speaking the term "Physically Challenged" means disadvantage for a given individual, resulting from an impairment of disability that prevents of restricts the fulfillment of a role that is normal (depending on the sex and social cultural factors) for the individual. According to World Health Organisation a "Physically Challenged Person" is one who has "impairment, *i.e.*, any loss or abnormality of psychological, physiological, anatomical structure of function." The disability can be by birth or can be caused by accident or due to malnutrition and other unhygienic conditions.

Librarians possess a very important position not only in the libraries but also in the parent organizations as well. They are mediators between the users and the collection of the library. They are the ones who know what user wants and how the documents can be fully used.

3. Objectives of the Study

1. Infrastructure for library services to persons with hearing disability.
2. Library staff and collections of libraries providing services to these persons.
3. Assistive technologies available and used for providing library services.

4. Review of Literature

Kumbier and Sarkey (2016) realized that the persons with disabilities must be able to move with no restrictions in the library building and stack areas. They further suggest that the toilets and work desks should be designed with a view to compatible with disabled. Grassi (2018) suggests a number of strategies as best and effective services for enrolled teens with disabilities, which include direct communications with teens with development of print reports with notable concern of privacy of disabled teens, encouragement of independence along with accepting inputs and advocating them to participate in programmes with permission granted. Actually, Grassi rightly frames various strategies to bring disabled teens in a streamline for better involvement of regular day to day activities for removing mental barriers in the mind of society towards disabled teens. In an interesting website- based survey, Liu *et al.* (2019) investigate websites of 129 public libraries to evaluate information services provided by them to the persons with disabilities. The study finds that most of the library websites are not suitable to provide information to person with disabilities. In a very surprising outcome, they notice that only seven libraries are compatible with programming in their websites to support disabled. The study also stresses over to train the staff for best and efficient services rendered to the persons with disabilities. Ayoung, D. A., Baada, F. N.A. and Baayel, P. (2021) in their study on disability laws at Ghana, suggest that the government/state institutions must be well equipped for implementing the amended laws supporting persons with disability in Ghana. They further recommend that the funding of the libraries for enhancing support services to disabled must be instituted separately.

5. Library Building

It is generally recognized that access to the library is a vital issue to be considered by the service providers to the persons with hearing disability. They shall be discouraged from using the library altogether if there are too many barriers to access the same. So the library buildings should have modifications like proper signage, talking signage and elevators, ramps, *etc.* to provide the users with the physical access to the library building freely and conveniently. The libraries are generally should not be housed in a single room with no facilities. These should have proper lighting and ventilation therein. These libraries should not be located on the top floors and even in the basements.

If the main entrance is not accessible approachable for disabled users, an alternative entrance, equipped with automatic senor based doors r, a ramp, and a telephone should be provided. There should be proper parking spaces near the entrance of the library, marked with the international symbol for the disabled should be provided/reserved for the hearing impaired Persons who come to avail of the library services there. The displays, signposting, *etc.* should be clear and easy to read there.

6. Access to the Library Materials and Services by Hearing Impaired Users

The libraries for such type of special users should be fully accessible. There should be logical arrangement of the library space with proper clear cut signage and floor plans depicted at the entrance and different corners and sections of the library. The information desk should be located near the entrance. Wheelchairs should be made available to move around inside all parts/sections of the whole library. Instead of doorsteps, ramps should be provided and all doors should have automatic opening and closing technology. The users should be able to reach book shelves using wheelchairs and also have proper signage for list of documents available. Some tables and computers should be reserved/dedicated for persons with such disabilities. At least one reserved toilet for disabled should be there.

7. Staff of the Libraries

The library staff plays a very important role in providing services to the persons with hearing disabilities. The qualification, training and skills of the staff assigned for providing services to such special kind of the library users is an indicator of the quality of the services provided therein, as well as an indicator of the level of organizational support for providing library services to these special users.. The staff required in the libraries can be categorized as "Professional Staff" and "Supporting Staff". The "Supporting Staff" may also be called a "Semi-professional" or "Non-Professional" staff. The libraries serving the persons with hearing disability are different from those serving the normal persons. They differ not only in terms of users they serve but also in terms of services, equipments and reading material. To cope up with these changes, the professional staff of the library requires special training to provide specialized services to their clients. The staff familiar with collections of the library helps in fulfilling the needs of the users by selecting the material as per their requirements is known as "Reader's Service" which should be available in libraries serving the persons with hearing disability.

8. Library Collection

A library's collection is very important part of its services and a reflection of its mission. Having a good collection for providing quality services to such special users is very important aspect of any library. The persons with hearing disability are equally diverse clientele with same reading needs as those of any other group. They require collection that includes popular magazines, information on course work, jobs, etc. the collection should support the reading needs of all ages of the disabled person's right from the children to the adults. They also need appropriate formats or aid to help them to access their required information. The alternative formats include e-books, audio cassettes or CD and other formats include assistive software. They need recreational reading, educational materials, encyclopedias, directories and all other kinds of documents, which are used by the normal people. Although the magazines and newspapers are available in all the libraries, a very small percentage of libraries have these in alternative format i.e. in electronic form or audio format. The number of periodicals and newspapers subscribed by the libraries are the measures often used to compare the size of the library. Nowadays these are available in alternative formats i.e. e-newspaper, talking newspapers, digital, *etc*.

There is a range of equipments, which can be used for accessing information from the library. These range from photocopying machines to closed circuit television cameras capable of magnifying. They can read the text aloud and can employ scanner for generating a file for use with the help of the computer.

9. Library Services

The libraries play a very important role in providing services to the person with hearing disability. The library may be of any type i.e. public, academic, or special, the services and operations of all these are aimed at providing information to the users. The information is disseminated through the services provided by the libraries. Hence the libraries are required to plan their services very carefully, taking into consideration the needs of these groups of users. These persons can avail the library services through postal service, mobile, email, fax, *etc.* while sitting at their places. Postal and mobile services are important for house bound adults.

All the library services must identify the needs, develop policies, resources, services keeping view the needs of the hearing impaired users. No library service is self sufficient, either in the range of subjects covered or in the books on its shelves. Therefore, Inter Library Lending between libraries has been a long established practice. The libraries function as a part of wider network providing better library services. These services help the PCP to access the information in desired formats.

Online Library Catalogue is one of the important sources of information for providing services to the users. The libraries should provide training to use assistive devices to these users. Different libraries adopt different methods for promoting these services, these services should be provided in according to the needs of these users. The libraries have to select the reading material for developing the collection. The material should be selected on the basis of criteria, which should reflect the needs of this community and should be balanced to meet their subject, recreational or information needs

10. Circulation and Reference Desk

Since these users are required to get the documents issued for use at home also, the circulation desk should have the following facilities:

i) Adjustable information kiosk/desk;

ii) Latest state of the art technology for hearing impaired persons;

iii) Facility of seating arrangement for elderly and disabled persons;

iv) Self-service and smart check in and checkout stations

11. Library Users with Hearing Impairment

The users with hearing disabilities are in need of special attention when they come to the libraries. The library staff should have the training to handle the patrons with these disabilities. Documents and information specifically for the persons with hearing disabilities should be easy to locate and users should feel comfortable in doing so. The following steps should be taken to help the library users having reading, hearing and other physical disabilities:

i) A specially designed section/room with talking books and other materials for the persons with reading disabilities should be established/earmarked;
ii) A special colored line/signage/arrows leading to this special department should be provided;
iii) Proper and clear signs with lights should be displayed
iv) Provision of comfortable seating area with bright reading light should be there

12. State of the Art Computers

Computers for such special library users should be made available/reserved. Provision of Technical support should be there for both computers and assistive equipments fro hearing impaired users. The library staff should be able to handle and provide on-site support. Necessary steps should be taken to ensure the following facilities:

i) A tape recorder, CD player, Digital Audio Information System (DAISY), palmtops and other equipment to complement the audiovisual collection should be made available;
ii) Electronic readers like palm tops, headphones or audio CSs should be provided.

13. Telecommunication Devices for the Deaf (TDD)

It is a type of text telephone which is connected to other set of telephone for sending typed messages to each other over telephone lines to other individual having TDDs. This is about the size of a typewriter or laptop with a QWERTY keyboard and small screen that uses LED or an LCD screen to display typed text electronically. In addition, a small spool of paper is also attached on which text is also printed. The text is transmitted live, via a telephone line, to a compatible device.

14. Tele-typewriters (TTYs)

It is device the helps the hearing impaired to communicate with others having the similar disability through a telephone system known as TTYs. It looks similar to an electronic typewriter and has a display screen, this device transmits and receives electronic signals which the TTY converts to text and displays it on the screen. The size of the display screen varies from 20 to 40 characters depending upon the type of device.

If some hearing impaired user not having this device and wishes to communicate with someone having this device, he will have to use the Relay service to call him or in some of the cases the computers are programmed to have communication with TTY device with proper transmission mode and computer has modem for the this purpose.

15. Captioning

Captioning is the process for converting audio into text and displaying the text on a screen or monitor. It provides on screen information to hearing impaired persons and is very helpful tool for the libraries providing such facilities. The hearing impaired users can make and receive phone calls using this technology. In case of communication, everything gets displayed on the respective screens. Calls are made like normal telephone call with special monitors attached for this purpose. It is useful for hearing impaired people, but at the same time they can talk and read captions clearly.

16. i Communicator

i Communicator is an amazing tool that can be use in libraries for enabling the users with hearing disability to communicate easily. It acts as alternate/ replacement to a sign language interpreter, in case of non availability of interpreter, for example special libraries, classrooms, daily communication, emergency situations etc. It is also known as real time translator and it translates: Speech to Text, Speech/Text to Video Sign-Language, Speech/Text to Computer generated voice.

17. Digital ALD's

Digital assistive listening systems are the latest devices available in the market. They are totally wireless and are easy to use. They connect directly to digital hearing aids using wi-fi or bluetooth technology, and are considered superior. Hearing disabled users who want to use a digital system can use it or the libraries can also use such devices for providing better experience to hearing impaired users.

18. Remote Video Conference Sign Language Interpreting using Skype

Many hearing impaired persons who use/understand sign language can take help of sign language interpreters through the internet using Skype. All that is required is a laptop or desktop computer with a fast internet connection. This is useful, particularly for people who are hearing diabled and reside in rural areas where access to sign language interpreters is limited. Skype is a form of video-conferencing using a webcam on the computer, laptop, TV, iPad, iPhone or iPod Touch with WiFi or 3g / 4G access. It can also be used for instant messaging.

19. Touch Screens

A touch screen is a computer display screen that is sensitive to human touch, allowing a user to interact with the computer by touching an active area, target or control such as pictures or words on the screen. Touch screens are activated by the insertion or removal of the fingertip or by pressing the controls active areas or targets with a mouth-stick, head-stick, or other similar device (stylus).

20. Voice Recognition Software

Voice recognition enables the user to enter text and, in some cases, carry out common computer tasks simply by speaking into a microphone, without using a keyboard or a mouse. While entering the text, the computer analyses the user's voice, recognize the words, and types these - instead of the user - as he or she speaks. This is used to bypass the keyboard and just speak infront of the computer. By programming the computer with a set of predefined instructions/commands, the user can control the computer by verbally issuing commands into a microphone.

21. Virtual Mouse

It is graphical on screen mouse, virtual mouse, having all the functions of standard mouse which is used with the computers. It is a type of software programme for special type of users.

22. Single Purpose Assistive Listening Systems

A Pocket Talker is a personal listening system that can be helpful in one-on-one situations. A wire connects the transmitter to the receiver so the speaker must be positioned close to the listener and neither can move around. A Hearing Aid Telephone Interconnect System (HATIS) is an assistive listening device for a telephone. One part plugs into the audio jack of the phone, and the other part is placed over a hearing aid.

23. Assistance from the Government

Library is a growing organism and no library is self- sufficient. It depends on the assistance from various sources for providing appropriate services to its users. The libraries serving the hearing impaired require more help as they are facing paucity of funds as well as scarcity of the skilled manpower. The libraries can improve the quality of library services to these users with the help of Government as well as Non Government Organizations. The Government can help the libraries in two ways, firstly, by laying down standards for providing services and issuing instructions to the concerned libraries and secondly by providing timely grants for improving the financial health of libraries.

24. Conclusion

The assistive technology is considered and has been an important aspect for the social inclusion of the disabled people in the society.. Thereby playing a significant role in terms of choice and opportunity for the disabled people in accessing the information from the libraries, thereby creating a barrier free environment.. It has also been identified as playing a significant role in offering severely disabled people an increased degree of independence in everyday life.

The problems faced by the Library Authorities in running the libraries for person with hearing impairment like paucity of funds, lack of staff, etc. are of trivial nature and can be overcome with little interest, enthusiasm and motivation. Regular funds from the Government will also enhance the quality of library services to the person with hearing impairment. These steps will help in establishing a well equipped library in every institution meant for the .hearing impaired persons.

References

Ayoung, D. A., Baada, F. N.-A., & Baayel, P. (2021). Access to library services and facilities by persons with disability: Insights from academic libraries in Ghana. *Journal of Librarianship and Information Science*, 53(1), 167–180. https://doi.org/10.1177/0961000620917723

Bae, K.J., Jeong, Y.S., Shim, W.S., & Kwak, S.J. (2007). The ubiquitous library for blind and physically handicapped: a case study of LG Sangnam Library, Korea. *IFLA Journal*, 33(3), 210-19.

Cylke, F. K., Moodie, M. M., & Fistick, R. E. (2007). Serving the blind and the physically handicapped in the United States of America. *Library Trends*, 55(4),796-808.

Fischer, A. (2005). National library service for the blind and physically handicapped. *Library of Congress Information Bulletin*, 64(1),10.

Grassi, R. (2018). Building inclusive communities: teens with disabilities in libraries. *Reference Services Review*, 46(3), 364-378.

Hill H. (2013). Disability and accessibility in the library and information science literature: A content analysis. *Library and Information Science Research*, 35(2),137–142.

Koulikordi, Anna (2008), Library services for people with disabilities in Greece. *Library Review*, 57(2), 138- 148.

Kumbier, A., & Starkey, J. (2016). Access is not problem-solving: Disability justice and libraries. Library Trends, 64(3), 468–491.

Panella, Nancy. (2009). The library services to the people with special needs section of IFLA: An historical overview. *IFLA Journal*, 35(3), 258-71.

16

Making Scientometric Portrait of Historian Romila Thapar

Pranjal Deka[1] and Monjit Gogoi[2]

[1]Government Model College, Kaziranga, Golaghat, Assam – 785 609

[2]Department of History, Government Model College, Kaziranga Golaghat, Assam – 785 609

ABSTRACTS

Historiography deals with the idea of history writing in different timeframe in different environments and in this discourse historian plays significant role. Indian ancient past is a fertile ground to understand different socio-political aspects of the country from various standpoints. Remaining within the paradigm of historiography historian like Romila Thapar not only emphasizing to understand the past but also tries to disseminate these through their writings in different scholarly platform. Apart from her valuable writings in the form of books, her writings in different reputed journals also impress sizable generations of new scholars. In this study an attempt has been made to study her contribution in intellectual field through writing history of Indian past.

Keywords: History, Historian, Romila Thapar, Past, Historiography.

1. Introduction

India has a prolong tradition of keeping their past in the form of history. From ancient period onwards history has been treated as an important subject to understand their recent past therefore, special treatment was being given to the historians for their endeavor. This trend had also been noticed in subsequent periods. However, considering the importance of history writing and historian, a new trend of study of history writings or historiography has also been developed in India. In his book "What is history" E.H. Carr rightly says about the importance of this new trend of historiography by considering History as an unending dialogue between past and present. Romila Thapar, a prominent historian of India not only highlights various issues of ancient past rather she challenge existing theories through her writings which enormously widened the historical horizon of ancient past. In this study an attempt has been made to understand her scholarly endeavors in different journals.

Romila Thapar's book "Asoka and the Decline of the Mauryas" is an important scholarly works which deals with the representation of history of Mauryas in general and policies of Emperor Asoka in particular. In her discussion she highlights various aspects of Dhamma policy adopted by king Ashoka and importance of centralize administration at that point of time.

Table-1: Top Ten cited Paper of Romila Thapar (From Scopus database)

So. No.	Year	Title	Source title	Vol.	Issue	Page start	Page end	Cited by
1.	1989	Imagined Religious Communities? Ancient History and the Modern Search for a Hindu Identity	Modern Asian Studies	23	2	209	231	184
2.	1971	The Image of the Barbarian in Early India	Comparative Studies in Society and History	13	4	408	436	41
3.	2012	From Lineage to State: Social Formations of the Mid-First Millenium BC in the Ganga Valley	From Lineage to State: Social Formations of the Mid-First Millenium BC in the Ganga Valley			1	198	36
4.	2009	The history debate and school text books in India: A personal memoir	History Workshop Journal	67	1	87	98	20
5.	1992	Black gold: South Asia and the roman maritime trade	South Asia: Journal of South Asia Studies	15	2	1	27	15
6.	1991	Genealogical Patterns as Perceptions of the Past	Studies In History	7	1	1	36	11
7.	2001	Perceiving the Forest: Early India	Studies in History	17	1	1	16	10
8.	2006	The mauryan empire in early India	Historical Research	79	205	287	305	6
9.	1975	A Possible Identification of Meluhha, Dilmun and Makan*)	Journal of the Economic and Social History of the Orient	18	3-Jan	1	42	6
	2005	Politics: Politics and the rewriting of history in India	Critical Quarterly	47	2-Jan	195	203	5

Similarly her another scholarly work "History of India Vol 1" is an interesting literary work to understand various aspects of ancient Indian history from 1500 B.C to the arrival of Europeans. Thapar's ideas and understanding on social life of ancient India was reflected in her work Ancient Indian Social History. Apart from above mentioned works, her endeavor to understand the state formation process in the middle Ganga valley in first millennium B.C and the whole question of transition of economy reflected in her work "From Lineage to State".

Moreover, Early India, The past as Present, The Past before Us: Historical Traditions of Early *North India* and other scholarly works making a noteworthy contribution in the historiographic development of India. Since this paper is about to study her works in various reputed journals using various databases therefore table-1 represents her top cited ten publications in different scholarly platform.

2. Collaborating Organizations

Romila Thapar has done lots of works with different scholarly organizations of all over the country and across the globe. These works reflects intellectual strength of Romila Thapar in the domain of historiography. Following figure testifies the collaborating works of Romila Tahpar with different organizations.

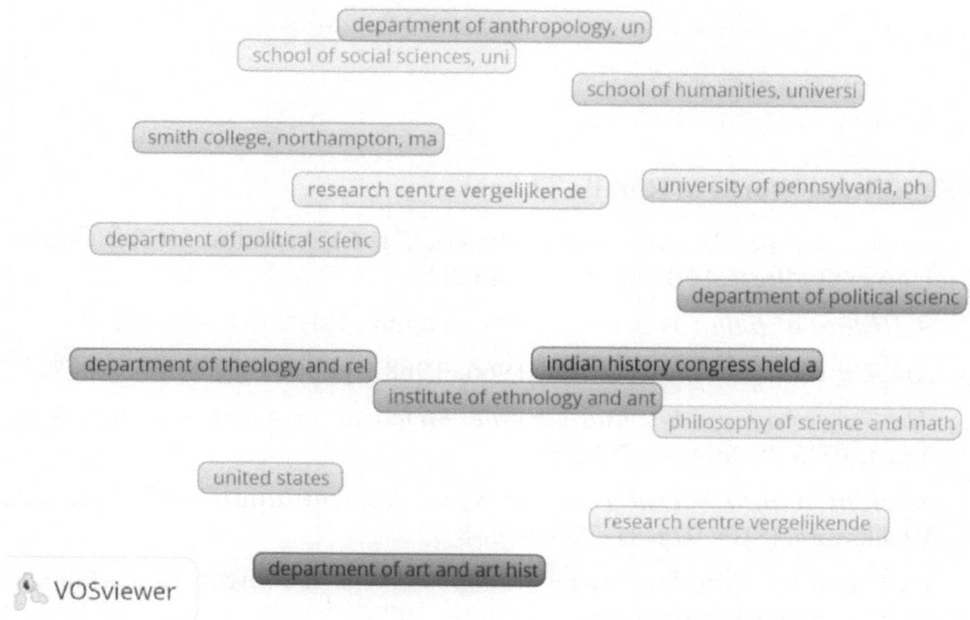

Fig. 1: Collaborating Organizations

3. Top Co-authors of Romila Thapar

Romila Thapar has done various works with co-authors of different places and some of them are being highlighting in the following figure.

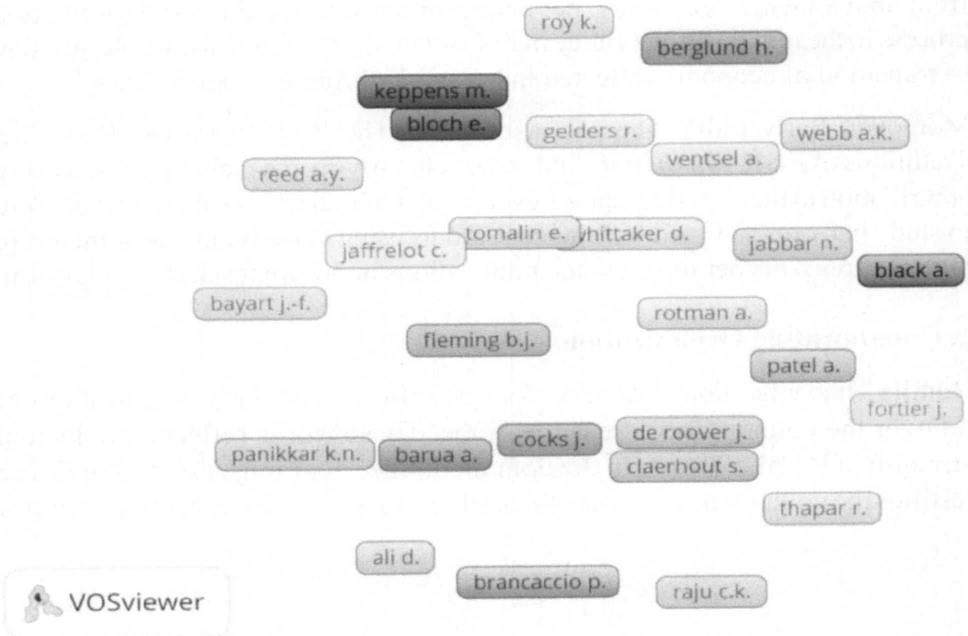

Fig. 2: Top Co Author

4. Significant Works of Romila Thapar

- *Aœoka and the Decline of the Mauryas*, 1961 (revision 1998); Oxford University Press, ISBN 0-19-564445-X
- *A History of India: Volume 1*, 1966; Penguin, ISBN 0-14-013835-8
- *Ancient India, Medieval India*, 1966, 1968 sq.; NCERT Textbooks[6]
- *The Past and Prejudice (Sardar Patel Memorial Lectures)*, National Book Trust, 1975, ISBN 81-237-0639-1
- *Ancient Indian Social History: Some Interpretations*, 1978, Orient Blackswan, ISBN 978-81-250-0808-8
- *Exile and the Kingdom: Some Thoughts on the Râmâyana*, Rao Bahadur R. Narasimhachar Endowment lecture, 1978;[25]
- *Dissent in the Early Indian Tradition*, Volume 7 of M.N. Roy memorial lecture, 1979; Indian Renaissance Institute[26]

- *From Lineage to State: Social Formations of the Mid-First Millennium B.C. in the Ganges Valley*, 1985; Oxford University Press (OUP), ISBN 978-0-19-561394-0
- *The Mauryas Revisited*, Sakharam Ganesh Deuskar lectures on Indian history, 1987; K.P. Bagchi & Co., ISBN 978-81-7074-021-6
- *Interpreting Early India*, 1992 (2nd edition 1999); Oxford University Press 1999, ISBN 0-19-563342-3
- *Cultural Transaction and Early India: Tradition and Patronage*, Two Lectures, 1994; OUP, ISBN 978-0-19-563364-1
- *Sakuntala: Texts, Readings, Histories*, 2002; Anthem, ISBN 1-84331-026-0
- *History and Beyond*, 2000; OUP, ISBN 978-0-19-566832-2
- *Cultural Pasts: Essays in Early Indian History*, 2003; OUP, ISBN 0-19-566487-6
- *Somanatha: The Many Voices of History*, 2005; Verso, ISBN 1-84467-020-1
- *India: Historical Beginnings and the Concept of the Aryan*, Essays by Thapar, et al., 2006; National Book Trust, ISBN 978-81-237-4779-8
- *The Aryan: Recasting Constructs*, Three Essays, 2008; Delhi, ISBN 978-81-88789-68-9
- *The Past before Us: Historical Traditions of Early North India*, 2013; Permanent Black, Harvard University Press, ISBN 978-0-674-72523-2
- *The Past As Present: Forging Contemporary Identities Through History*, 2014; Aleph, ISBN 93-83064-01-3
- *Communalism and the Writing of Indian History*, Romila Thapar, Harbans Mukhia, Bipan Chandra, 1969 People's Publishing House[27]
- *Situating Indian History: For Sarvepalli Gopal*, 1987; OUP, ISBN 978-0-19-561842-6
- *Indian Tales*, 1991; Puffin, ISBN 0-14-034811-5
- *India: Another Millennium?* 2000; Viking, ISBN 978-0-14-029883-3
- *Early India: From Origins to AD 1300*, 2002; Penguin, ISBN 0-520-23899-0

5. Conclusion

From the above discussion we can come to this conclusion that in the field of Indian historiography Romila Thapar is a noteworthy figure who makes valuable contribution in different fields of history through her scholarly works. In this study an attempt was being made to understand works of Romila Thapar using scientrometric tolls and this type of study could bring many historians and theirs works to massive public audience.

References

Kademani, B. S., Kalyane, V. L., & Balakrishnan, M. R. (1994). Scientometric portrait of PK Iyengar. *Library Science*, 31(4), 155-176.

Kademani, B. S., Kalyane, V. L., & Jange, S. (1999). Scientometric portrait of nobel laureate Dorothy Crowfoot Hodgkin. *Scientometrics*, 45(2), 233-250.

Kademani, B. S., Kalyane, V. L., & Kademani, A. B. (1994). Scientometric Portrait of Nobel Laureate Dr. CV Raman. *Indian Journal of Information, Library and Society*, 7(3-4), 215-249.

Kademani, B. S., Kalyane, V. L., & Kademani, A. B. (1996). Scientometric portrait of Nobel laureate S. Chandrasekhar. *JISSI: the International Journal of Scientometrics and Informetrics*, 2(2-3), 119-135.

Kademani, B. S., Kalyane, V. L., & Kumar, V. (2001). Scientometric portrait of nobel laureate Ahmed Hassan Zewail. *Malaysian Journal of Library & Information Science*, 6(2), 53-70.

Kalyane, V. L., & Kalyane, S. V. (1993). Scientometric portrait of Vinodini Reddy. *Journal of Information Sciences*, 4(1), 25-47.

Kalyane, V. L., & Kalyane, S. V. (1993). Scientometric portrait of Vinodini Reddy. *Journal of Information Sciences*, 4(1), 25-47.

Kalyane, V. L., Prakasan, E. R., & Kumar, V. (2001). Scientometric Portrait of Ranjit Kumar Mitra. *ILA Bulletin*, 37(2), 39-53.

Thapar, R. (1990). *A history of India*. Penguin UK.

Thapar, R. (1996). The theory of Aryan race and India: History and politics. *Social Scientist*, 3-29.

Thapar, R. (2000). Cultural pasts. *Essays in Early Indian History. New Delhi*.

Thapar, R. (2012). *Ashoka and the Decline of the Mauryas*. Oxford University Press.

Index

J

K

L

M

N

O

P